D0848097

this is the old english sheepdog

t.f.h.

joan mcdonald brearley

and marlene j. anderson

Cover—
A beautiful Old English Sheepdog owned by Priscilla Yager of Middlesex, New Jersey.

Frontispiece:
Eight Bobtails from the Merriedip Kennels owned by Mrs. Lewis Roesler of Great Barrington, Mass. and featured in an issue of *House and Garden* magazine many years ago. Photo by *House and Garden's* C. E. Harbison.

ISBN 0-87666-345-5

Distributed in the U.S.A. by T.F.H. Publications, Inc., 211 West Sylvania Avenue, P.O. Box 27, Neptune City, N.J. 07753; in England by T.F.H. (Gt. Britain) Ltd., 13 Nutley Lane, Reigate, Surrey; in Canada by Clarke, Irwin & Company, Clarwin House, 791 St. Clair Avenue West, Toronto 10, Ontario; in Southeast Asia by Y. W. Ong, 9 Lorong 36 Geylang, Singapore 14; in Australia and the south Pacific by Pet Imports Pty. Ltd., P.O. Box 149, Brookvale 2100, N.S.W., Australia.
Published by T.F.H. Publications, Inc. Ltd., The British Crown Colony of Hong Kong.

DEDICATION

The authors wish to dedicate this book to all those who revere the noble work done by Old English Sheepdogs over the years, who want to preserve their place in the world of dogs, to those who hold the integrity of the breed and its future above the mere winning in the show ring . . . and who love the breed best when it is a member of their family!

and to

Kate Lemonier

who knew the importance and meaning of such things.

CONTENTS

JOAN McDONALD BREARLEY

Joan Brearley has loved animals ever since she was old enough to know what they were. . . .

Over the years there has been a constant succession of dogs, cats, birds, fish, rabbits, snakes, turtles, alligators, squirrels, lizards, etc., for her own personal menagerie. Through these same years she has owned over thirty different breeds of purebred dogs, as well as countless mixtures, since the door was never closed to a needy or homeless animal.

A graduate of the American Academy of Dramatic Arts, Joan started her career as a writer for movie magazines, actress and dancer. She also studied journalism at Columbia University and has been a radio, TV, and magazine writer, writing for some of the major New York City agencies. She was also producer-director for a major network.

Her accomplishments in the dog fancy include being an American Kennel Club approved judge, breeder-exhibitor of top show dogs, writer for the various dog magazines, author of *This Is the Afghan Hound, The Samoyed,* and co-author of *This Is the Shih Tzu, This is the Saint Bernard,* and *This is the Bichon Frise.* For five years she was Executive Vice-President of the Popular Dogs Publishing Company and editor of *Popular Dogs* magazine, the national prestige publication for the dog fancy at that time.

Joan is just as active in the cat fancy, and in almost all the same capacities. She is most interested in animal legislation and is the editor of the Cat Fanciers Association, Inc. Yearbook. She speaks at kennel clubs and humane organizations and has received many awards and citations for her work in this field, including an award from the Morris Animal Foundation in Denver. She is also a contributor on animals to the *World Book Encyclopedia.*

At present Joan lives in a penthouse apartment overlooking Manhattan in New York City with an Old English Sheepdog,

Afghan Hound, Shih Tzu, Cavalier King Charles Spaniel and a dozen or more cats, all of which are Best in Show winners and have been professional models for television and magazines. Joan has the rare distinction of having bred a Westminster Kennel Club group winner in her first litter of Afghan Hounds, Champion Sahadi (her kennel prefix) Shikari, the top winning Afghan Hound in the history of the breed.

In addition to her activities in the world of animals, Joan Brearley is a movie buff and spends time at the art and auction galleries, the theatre, creating needlepoint (for which she has also won awards), dancing, the typewriter—and the zoo!

MARLENE J. ANDERSON

Marlene Anderson was born into a family of dog breeders. She grew up in the dog business, surrounded by many breeds, which her mother and grandmother successfully raised. Young Marlene helped with the management of a large boarding and breeding kennel. It soon became the subject about which she knew most. Her grandmother's favorite dog was the Saint Bernard and she always kept some magnificent specimens of the breed. Thus, Marlene's constant companions were Saints and, along with her Old English Sheepdogs, still are today. The Beau Cheval Kennels also breed Mastiffs and Briards as well.

Having a background in many arts, she joined the United States Air Force when she was 18 to work in Special Services. There she met and married Douglas J. Anderson when she was 20. She left the service several months later, and soon afterward became seriously ill. After a long stay in a hospital, close to death, doctors finally diagnosed her disease as the dreaded and hopeless multiple sclerosis. With the impending doom of life in a wheelchair threatening her, Marlene's doctors prescribed a hobby or business that would keep her hands busy and her mind occupied. Her husband left the service, where he had been a career man, and the couple decided to raise dogs.

After they had traveled around the country a bit, with a brief stay in Alaska, their first daughter was born and the Andersons moved to the wilds of Western Maryland, where Beau Cheval Kennels was established in 1957.

While Douglas worked far away from home and was gone for weeks at a time, Marlene busied herself gathering stock, studying Standards and working with dogs. German Shepherds were Douglas' favorite at the time and they were the breed decided upon. The little kennel shortly was filled with them. Although Marlene liked Shepherds, too, soon other breeds were added—Dachshunds, Pekingese, Saint Bernards and Old English Sheep-

dogs! They began breeding Saints in 1961 and the Bobtails shortly thereafter.

Moving to Western Pennsylvania about that time to be closer to Douglas' work, the couple became interested in dog shows. On one occasion, they were invited by another breeder to enter a show to build points so that the other breeder's dog could finish.

Douglas won a four-point major that first time he walked into the show ring, and both he and Marlene were hooked! Since that time the Andersons have bred or owned 50 champions of record, none of which was purchased as a champion, nor with any points; most were bred by Marlene.

The family later moved to Bucks County, Pennsylvania, to be closer to the East's largest and most competitive dog shows.

Now, as the mother of four healthy daughters, Marlene feels the doctors were evidently wrong about the disease they diagnosed years ago.

The Andersons' goal has always been to better themselves, their environment, and their dogs. Never satisfied with what they produce, they constantly strive to breed better dogs. Marlene believes common sense is the secret ingredient necessary in any venture, and especially in the mad, wonderful game of breeding and showing dogs!

CHAPTER 1

HISTORY OF THE BREED

The history of the Old English Sheepdog is difficult to trace and thus remains a bit of a mystery. About two hundred years ago when the Old English Sheepdog was coming into its own as an individual breed, pedigrees were neither highly regarded nor recorded at all! Breeding was based on *the requirements of a good working dog* rather than on a purebred strain, and eventually each country that used dogs for herding seemed to have its own version of a sheepdog. What the Collie was to Scotland, the Old English Sheepdog was to England, and strangely enough, their working requisites were very similar.

As far away as Russia the sheepdogs also bore a strong resemblance. If the size was reduced and the tail "bobbed," the Russian Owtchah was very much like the Old English Sheepdog. It was a large dog, blue grizzled or blue merled in color, and carried a similar coat. The Briard also bears a strong resemblance. Perhaps the strongest resemblance of all is to the Bearded Collie. . . . really remarkable look-alikes in the canine world!

The Hungarian Kuvasz also can be included among the look-alikes. It is uniformly white, however, and a larger, more powerful dog. But it is equally faithful, distrustful of strangers, and potentially dangerous to trespassers, all attributes we claim for our Old English Sheepdog. The Giant Himalayan was another large dog which was employed to attack wolves which went after sheep, as was the Armant.

The Armant took its name from a town in Egypt. While from yet another continent, in actuality its conformation was very much like that of the Briard, or the Chien de Brie, the lovely French sheepdog which was taken from Corsica to Egypt during Napoleon's Egyptian expedition. In Egypt the Armant is sometimes referred to as the Egyptian Sheepdog; it can definitely be considered to be a relative of the Old English Sheepdog.

The first Armant to reach England belonged to the Egyptian minister, H. E. Pasha. The dog was also called Ermenti or Sabe, which are Arabic words meaning lion. The body of the Armant was also square and the tail was docked. Its coat was long and shaggy, and tangled easily. Colors varied slightly, but sizes and heights of Armants were comparable to those of the Old English Sheepdog.

The Welsh also claimed the Old English Sheepdog as their own. However, even though some Welsh heelers had lived in England for generations, it was proved by a Mr. Edward Lloyd over the years that they originally came from the South Downs of Sussex, England.

So while we know that the Old English Sheepdog goes back about two hundred years, we still cannot call it an ancient breed. Only herding dogs have been around since man first needed and used them for such purposes. The original herders were probably the Mastiffs, or Mastiff-like dogs, since in the early times an even stronger, heavier and more powerful animal was needed to fend off all sorts and sizes of attackers. They were courageous animals and wore heavy collars covering the entire neck. The collars were usually studded with spikes or prongs, since the wolf attacks the throat of its victims, and wolves remained the major concern of the herdsmen.

Many countries used dogs for herding both sheep and cattle. And it was only when wolves became less numerous that the smaller, lighter sheepdogs were gradually developed and utilized in the fields. A gentle, intelligent dog was needed to drive the cattle and sheep from town to town for sale or for slaughter; good herding dogs not only had to stay on the job but also had to possess good hearing, sharp sight, tracking ability and a loud bark to do the job well. It was this intelligence and insight, together with their speed, agility and endurance, which made the good sheepdogs so in demand.

The Old English Sheepdog as we know it today had only become popular in England by the 1800's, when owners began to breed almost exclusively for intelligence, speed and endurance. Those dogs which showed no marked ability in working or obeying commands were culled early. Today's Old English still have—or should have—these innate herding instincts.

All of us have watched them herd children, cats, chickens and ducks, and even people, whenever they get the chance! Many new Sheepdog owners think that the nip they get on their thigh from their Sheepdog means he has a mean streak. NOT SO! He is simply trying to keep you in line! Hopefully it will be the children he keeps in line, but nevertheless you should know he is a trusted and dependable babysitter, inside or outside the house, and that he is thinking and behaving as a true Old English Sheepdog should.

Many owners report that their Old English Sheepdogs have started herding sheep or cattle as late in life as eight or ten years of age, even though they have not been reared on a farm or exposed to livestock before.

Being shaggy and compactly built, the Old English Sheepdog has always elicited comparisons to the teddy bear. He has also been talked about in dog circles because of his bobbed tail.

While it is known that most sheepdogs are born WITH tails (which are docked at the first joint sometime during the first five days of life), there are those who claim to breed litters in which one or more pups are born without tails, or with short tails. Those who claim Old English Sheepdog ancestry going back to the Bearded Collie are the first to tell you that the only difference between the two is the tail and that it is generally a matter of amputation.

The reasons for the tailless Sheepdog are both practical and interesting. The bobbed tail is believed to have been done primarily so that the tax collectors would recognize the dog as a worker and therefore not subject its owner to Inland Revenue taxation! And those who have ever had an Old English know that the bobbed tail also is helpful in keeping the animal's hindquarters clean. This cleanliness was also the reason the tails of the sheep they herded were also cropped—to prevent the excessive coat in this area from becoming matted with excrement or mud.

The bobbed tail also gives the Sheepdog itself somewhat the look of the sheep so that it blends in well with the flock, thus fooling the wolves watching and following closely behind or gazing down on the herd from surrounding hills.

While the Old English Sheepdog does possess instinctive herding ability, it would take a patient trainer to take on an Old English Sheepdog for this work today. It is much easier for a young dog to watch or follow the lead of an older dog in an apprenticeship as he performs his work in the fields, and there just are not that many herding dogs around today.

The experienced herding dog must round up sheep scattered over many acres or square miles of farmlands. The Sheepdog must gather them together and drive them into a fold and then hold them there. He must circle wide and quietly, taking care not to frighten them, since animals panic easily and may stampede.

Heading dogs lead the sheep while hunt-away dogs seek out the stragglers from the herds. In Scotland and England, where sheep are driven in high country, an unintelligent or inexperienced dog might drive all the flock downhill, over the cliffs and into the sea. So you can see the importance of the stable dog which knows not only how to herd but also where and when not to use his bark. Sometimes these dogs actually jump onto the backs of the clustered sheep in the herds and walk across a sea of wool to take a short cut to the other side of the herd!

The dogs are directed by the shepherds or herders through basic commands, both audible and by silent arm signals, sometimes from great distances. The silent whistle has also been employed in some cases with impressive results.

The Sheepdog is essential to a shepherd and is often his best friend and constant companion for months at a time. A shepherd and his dog are usually good company for each other; the legends and stories which have come down through the years about these uncanny relationships and acts of intelligence and heroism on the part of the Old English Sheepdogs seem at times to be almost beyond belief . . . including the stories about the dogs which know their owners by mention of their name as well as by scent.

There is no doubt about the great bond which develops between the shepherds and their dogs, all of which give credence to the claim that the Old English Sheepdog is the ideal dog for work or for fun. It was this remarkable two-way friendship that prompted Aubrey Hopwood in 1905 to write in his Old English Sheepdog book, ". . . there are few companions, even human, of whom you can expect as much, and get it!"

The Old English Sheepdog as it was rendered in an oil painting by Philip Reinagle (1749-1833).

As the Old English Sheepdog began to establish itself as a breed unto itself during the 1800's, we notice also that more and more artists of that period were beginning to portray the dogs in their paintings. In Gainsborough's 1771 painting of the Duke of Buccleuch, the Duke holds in his arms a good dog believed to be an Old English Sheepdog puppy. Then there was the Mathew Dixon painting of *The Duke of Grafton as A Boy*. Other artists such as Cooper, Bewick and Philip Reinagle also painted the Old English into their works around the turn of the century.

It was in 1880 that the English breed club was founded. The first exhibition of the breed was in 1873 at Curzon Hall at the Birmingham Dog Show, where there were three entered. The breed generated a great deal of interest at the shows, and the British began to think of the dog in a new light. In fact, by 1897, Dr. Edwardes-Ker had written of his concern regarding the possibility of losing the original characteristics of the breed by so much inbreeding for the sake of producing showier Sheepdogs. Though the larger dogs seemed to be preferred in the ring for their beauty and strength, the shepherds themselves around this time were beginning to keep the smaller specimens, since they not only ate less but also could dart about faster. Dr. Ker, considered an authority on the breed, having bred them for thirty years and having produced more Old English at his Dorchester location than were produced in any other part of England, foresaw even at this early stage the dangers of bad temperament and bad specimens as a result of the improper breeding. In a report to the club in 1897 he wrote ". . . Above all things let us beseech you Sheepdog breeders to avoid consanguinity and its consequent race of imbecile individuals, if your object and aim is to maintain that hardihood of nerve and limb which assists to form the essential characteristics of this picturesque and rugged breed." Needless to say, many of the magnificent showdogs of today do not necessarily look like the herding drovers of yesterday . . . so Dr. Ker's predictions of things to come were not totally unfounded!

Dr. Ker was not the only one who had reservations about the new turn in the career of the Old English Sheepdog. In 1899, in a new edition of *Modern Dogs*, a Mr. Rawdon Lee wrote, "Within the past few years the bob-tailed sheep dog has become much popularized, and at many of the South Country shows several classes are provided which invariably attract good entries. For instance, at the most recent show of the Kennel Club there were fifty entries; at a comparatively small show held at Streatham, Surrey, early in 1898, there were forty-six entries."

So despite all fears and premonitions, the Old English Sheepdog had endeared itself with the dog fancy and was firmly entrenched in the show world, where it would be from that day forward.

Most of the Old English Sheepdogs descended from four celebrated ancestors which came into prominence from fame won at those first dog show classes. These were Bentinck Bob and Champion Watchboy, whelped in 1890 and bred by R. Abbott. He gathered many important wins from 1892 through 1896, and his was a prominent name in many pedigrees. Then there were Grizzle Bob and a bitch named Dairymaid. While the breeder, date of birth and pedigree of Champion Dairymaid are unknown,

Famous artist and sculpturess Carol Moorland Marshall rendered this highly appealing model of the Old English Sheepdog for lovers of the breed. Miss Marshall's work in many breeds is available at Abercrombie and Fitch in New York City, to mention just one prestige store which carries her work.

she was an outstanding example of the breed and was known to have come from Surrey in 1891 into the possession of William G. Weaver. Though she died four years later, she was invincible in her day, with a list of wins to do her owner proud. She attained championships at the Kennel Club, at Birmingham, and the Crufts show in 1892 and 1893. Mr. Weaver, a founder of the Old English Sheepdog Club and an accredited judge of the breed, had the satisfaction of knowing that she had earned the distinction of being regarded as one of the best bitches in the history of the breed. The story of his purchase of this great bitch from a shepherd on the South Downs for thirty shillings and a pot of beer was a story often told. She produced several litters for her astute owner. One of these litters included a bitch named Little Nell, which was the first Old English Sheepdog to win a challenge certificate. She also distinguished herself by producing Champion Masterpiece, an Old English named Washington, and several others sired by the celebrated Wall-Eyed Bob.

Wall-Eyed Bob was another great specimen of the breed whose pedigree and breeder were unknown. Rumor had it that he once changed hands in an English pub for a sovereign and subsequently became the property of a Mr. J. Thomas. Later still he was owned by Mrs. Fare Fosse, a famous person in the breed at the time. Had the present-day championship requirements been established during his prime, he surely would have attained this status. Wall-Eyed Bob was exhibited at the Botanic Show in June of 1898; he then was said to be at least fifteen years of age and was still an excellent specimen. He died shortly thereafter but still in magnificent coat and healthy to the last!

It was from Wall-Eyed Bob and a bitch named Wall-Eyed Flo that this ocular "wall-eyed" characteristic has been transmitted down to some of our modern dogs. These wall-eyed dogs were most appreciated by the farmers of the day, since it was believed that wall-eyed dogs never lost their excellent eyesight.

We can see, then, that by the turn of the century a high standard of excellence had been established in the breed. It was also the heyday of a dog named Kirkdale Bango, a sable dog with white markings, which was one of the first of his color to come to the public eye. Some of the other early showdogs of note were Sir Guy, Sir Lucifer, Sir Lancelot, Mayor of Newport, Blue Dorothy,

American Dame Judith, Dame Margery, Sir Caradoc and a dog named Sir Cavendish. Champion Sir Cavendish was bred by Dr. Edwardes-Ker, who did so much to preserve size in the breed, and brought about the breeding of his Sir Caradoc to a bitch named Dame Ruth; the breeding produced the handsome Sir Cavendish on May 29th, 1887.

Sir Ethelwolf, owned by Mr. A. H. Megson, won a championship at Crufts in 1897, and was a dog of great fame at the time, along with Lady Cavendish, Merle Princess, Brave Tory, Invincible Mayor of Newport, Dame Elizabeth, Thunder Cloud, Bahadur, Norfolk Bob, King Kroonah, Lady Scaramouche, Dame Jessie Ursa Mayor, Orson Bouncer, Princess Dorothy, Jubilee Queen, Talford Tatters, Marie and Dame Barbara, all duly famous as well.

We cannot fail to recall the imprint left by Mr. E. Y. Butterworth's Champion Bouncing Lass, born on June 18th, 1899. Sired by Young Watch out of Peggy Primrose, she was a direct descendant of Watch Boy and will go down in history, as Dairymaid did, as one of the best bitches in the breed. She won her first three challenge certificates at Hinchley in 1901, at Manchester in 1902, and Aquarium in 1902 also.

When sold to Mr. Tilley she added championships at the Crystal Palace, Birmingham, Liverpool, Birkenhead, Crufts, Leamington and Richmond to her list as well. Needless to say, these were all prestige shows at the time, but she added to her impressive list by winning the Brewers and Lord Mayor's Cup at Birmingham in 1902. In twelve months she captured nine cups, eleven medals and over one hundred first prizes. This same year she took two firsts, a championship and the Vanderbilt Cup in New York. This was a performance she repeated in 1904.

In the early 1890's there was a great dog named Harkaway, whelped on June 8th, 1891, sired by the famous Grizzle Bob EX Rachel, and bred by Mr. J. Thomas. This dog became a great show dog when he became the property of a Mr. H. Dickson. Even more important and notable than his showmanship was Harkaway's excellent coat, a trait he passed on as a sire, to the point that his equally well-coated progeny were said to possess the "Harkaway coat."

By the end of the 1890's several excellent dogs were triggering the interest in the Old English as a show dog. Another was

Champion Victor Cavendish, whelped January 1st, 1897. The famous Watchboy sired both his parents and passed on many great qualities to this famous grandson, which he in turn was to pass on to his progeny. In addition to many top prizes, Victor Cavendish took forty-two first and twenty-five special prizes at twenty-eight shows, including the Old English Sheepdog Challenge Cup at the Old English Sheepdog Club's special shows on three separate occasions.

A famous and respected breeder at the turn of the century was Mrs. Fare Fosse, mentioned earlier in this chapter as the owner of Wall-Eyed Bob; her dogs became known by their "Weather" suffix. One of the most famous was her Champion Fair Weather, born in May, 1898. Fair Weather's debut was at the Crufts Show in 1899 at nine months of age, and she won everything for which she was eligible. She became a champion while just a little more than a year old and at two years of age had won over fifty first prizes and nine championships. She eventually had a record nineteen championships.

Fair Weather whelped four litters in addition to holding the record for prize-winning! Fair Weather was held in such esteem by the fancy that upon her death she was stuffed and exhibited at the Natural History Museum at Tring.

Another of Mrs. Fosse's famous Old English Sheepdogs was Champion Rough Weather, born on August 27th, 1900. While still a young dog he acquired over one hundred and fifty first and special prizes in the show ring and one Best Dog In Show win. His challenge certificates were won at Crufts in 1903, Kennel Club in 1903, and Botanic and Birmingham in 1904. The first three wins, made under three different judges, entitled him to his place on the Honourable List of Bobtail Champions at that time. Some of Mrs. Fosse's other famed dogs were Rough Rider, Betsy Day, Shepton Moonshine, Ch. Tip Top Weather, Glorious Weather and Ch. Moonshine Weather.

Another great bitch to come along at about this time was Champion Dolly Gray, born April 26th, 1901, and bred by Mr. F. H. Travis. Mr. Travis was known for his insistence upon proper blue color in the coat of the Old English Sheepdog. His Dolly Gray captured a number of wins in 1904 and was winner of the Crufts International Bowl for best Non-Sporting Dog in the show! She won over one hundred and thirty first prizes, two hundred special prizes and seven cups, and on nine occasions she was awarded a special prize for the best exhibit in the show.

Another breeder who attained fame in the breed was Mrs. Breakspear, whose dogs became famous. Among them were Ch. Faithful Tramp, Ch. Tommy Tuttlemouse, Ch. Wall-Eyed Bill, Ch. Thamara, Ch. Lucky Prince, Ch. Blue Stocking, Ch. Blue Knight, Ch. Hillgarth Blue Boy, Ch. Blue Coat and Ch. Newcote Blossom. Ch. Elkington Squire was a grandson of Ch. Tip Top Weather and the sire of many winners, including Ch. River Girl. Ch. Stoneybroke was the winner at Crufts in 1933.

These are some of the great dogs and the dedicated breeders who set the pattern for the popularity and elegance of the breed as we know it today. So well did they plant the seed of interest and admiration for this great shaggy dog that today we find Old English Sheepdogs all over Europe, including Scandinavia. Several breeders in Holland have produced valuable champions and fine specimens of our breed; Mrs. Backs, to name one, is world famous.

One thing is certain, and that is that no matter where the Old English Sheepdog appears it is loved and admired as both a working dog and as a trusted companion. We respect and revere its noble beginnings and can now proudly devote ourselves to preserving the nobility of its heritage and the dignity (paradoxically mixed with clownishness!) it brings to the dog fancy!

Some of the English breeders who have done so much for the breed are the Amberford Kennels of Mrs. J. A. Keeling, Chesterfield, Beauville; Miss V. Keeling, Matlock; the Beckington Kennels of Mrs. K. Givson, Wales; Bewkes, Misses Smailes and Knight in Surrey; Lt. Col. M. D. Lister's Bleakdown, Isle of Wight; Bluecote, Mr. W. J. Calvey, Somerset; Bluewave, Mrs. E. Rollo in Dorset; A. J. Baker's Bluemark in Glamorgan; Miss C. F. Workman's Bobbycroft at Stratford-on-Avon; and Mrs. W. Grillett's Boldwood, Cambridge.

Also well known in England are the Bridewell Kennels, and then the Broadwell Kennels of Mr. J. Wasley, in Gloucestershire. The Camaes Kennels of Mrs. J. D. James also are in Gloucestershire. There are the Danum Kennels of F. Brocklesby in Doncaster; Daphnis, owned by Mr. E. J. J. Minett, in Stafford; Duroya, Mrs. A. E. Woodiwiss, near Sheffield; the Ellinghurst

Old English Sheepdogs of Mrs. J. C. R. Chapman, near Bristol; Fairacres, owned by Mrs. E. M. Bloor, Shropshire; Fernville, the prefix of N. W. R. Harrison, near Sheffield; Gordale, owned by C. C. St. J. Stacey, in Somerset; Grendonfell, Mrs. I. F. Cooke, Warwickshire; the Greystoke Bobtails of Miss J. M. Back, Edinburgh; Hornash, owned by Mr. and Mrs. R. F. Mathews, in Kent, and Keandor Kennels of Mr. and Mrs. A. R. Wood, Rotherham.

We see also in show catalogues and written accounts of the breed the names of Loakes Park and Marksman; the London kennel named Lanseer, owned by Mr. and Mrs. W. Ashley; Knockanyln, owned by M. J. A. Muirhead in Renfrewshire; and Linnifold, owned by Mr. and Mrs. J. S. Mason. Accountings of the activity in the breed mention also such names as Mrs. H. Booth's, Marlay; Pearlston, owned by Miss P. M. Peart in Berkshire; Perrywood Reculver, owned by Mrs. and Miss A. G. Wilkinson in Hastings; Mrs. Heyward Pinehurst in Sussex; Squarefour Old English owned by Mrs. I. C. Nicol, Peeblesshire; Talmora, Mrs. S. M. Talbot's prefix, as well the names of Tansley, Watchers, Weirwood, Yasabel and Yeldhams.

Famous for their records in their own country, the following kennels are famous also by way of the records amassed in the United States on the top dogs which they exported to this country. Many of these great imports are pictured in this book and bear the kennel names of Dalcroy, Miss A. Lloyd's kennel name for her establishment in Lichfield; Farleydene, owned by Mr. G. Gooch, Kent; Littleparc, Mrs. E. Jackson, Cardiff; Pastelblue, Miss I. Webster; Shepton, Miss F. Tilley; Rollingsea, Mrs. J. R. Gould, Cornwall, and the well-known Prospectblue.

These English kennel names can be found behind the great Old English Sheepdogs on both continents and figure prominently in pedigrees of many of the top-winning dogs in America over the years.

OLD ENGLISH SHEEPDOG CLUBS IN ENGLAND

Northwestern Old English Sheepdog Club

Founded 1923

Secretary, Mrs. Woodiwiss
Hillfarm, Unstone, near Sheffield

Old English Sheepdog Club
Founded 1888
Secretary, Mrs. I. R. Lapwood
810 Kenton Lane, Harrow Weald, Middlesex

Old English Sheepdog Club of Scotland
Secretary, Mr. and Mrs. J. Nicol
Woodlands, Romano Bridge, West Linton, Peeblesshire

Southeastern Old English Sheepdog Club
Secretary, Mr. A. A. G. Akehurst
19 Waldenhurst Road, Saint Mary Cray, Kent

Kennel Club
1–4 Clarges Street, Piccadilly, London, W.1, England

There is also an Old English Sheepdog Club of Ireland.

CHAPTER 2

THE OLD ENGLISH SHEEPDOG COMES TO AMERICA

The first of our beloved Bobtails was imported to the U.S.A. around 1888; the breed's establishment in the hearts of American dog lovers was largely attributable to the enterprising Mr. William Wade of Hulton, Pennsylvania, and his friend, the philanthropist Andrew Carnegie. The sole intent of these two noble gentlemen was to place in the arms of every American dog lover a good and worthy working dog . . . preferably the Old English Sheepdog!

Through his friendship with Mr. Freeman Lloyd, Old English Sheepdog enthusiast, international judge, and perhaps the greatest authority on Working Dogs at the time, in 1889 William Wade managed to have published in *Turf, Field and Farm* a monograph titled "The Old English Sheepdog." *Turf, Field and Farm* was a sports magazine for which Mr. Lloyd reported, and he himself authored the monograph introducing the breed to the American dog fancy.

Together with his contributions to *National Geographic Magazine*, the monograph gave a great deal of valuable exposure in the press. Partly because of Mr. Wade's habit of depositing Old English Sheepdog puppies on the doorsteps of his friends (gratis, of course), this incomparable breed could not help but take hold of the hearts of the recipients, and without further delay the breed caught on in the United States as it waned in its native land. And it was only after its impact here, and subsequent export to other countries, that the interest in the Old English Sheepdog began to grow again in England.

It was this same Freeman Lloyd who judged the first class of Bobtails at the Westminster Kennel Club show in 1903, which

One of the most colorful and important personalities in all of dogdom, Mr. Freeman Lloyd, who compiled and wrote *The Old English Sheepdog*, which William Wade of Hulton, Pennsylvania, published as a contribution to the breed at his own expense in 1889. Mr. Lloyd was Kennel Editor of *Field and Stream* magazine up until the time of his retirement and was a frequent contributor to *The National Geographic Magazine*. His series of articles on dogs which appeared in the first half of the century were influential in presenting purebred dogs to the public. A Percy Jones photograph.

brought out the first large class of Old English Sheepdogs in America. Mr. Henry Arthur Tilley, who was later to found the parent club, brought out an imported team of Old English Sheepdogs especially for competition at this show. In fact, many of the dogs brought over for this show were sold here to prominent people who helped to establish the breed.

Most notable among them perhaps was the well-known theatrical producer Charles Dillingham. It was Mr. Dillingham's stock, which was later sold to very wealthy Reginald Vanderbilt (of the Newport, Rhode Island, Vanderbilts) that produced and established the white-headed, blue-bodied Bobtails which did all the winning during the 1930's.

Unquestionably, however, the major contributor to establishing the breed was the dedicated Mrs. Edward Renner. Mrs. Renner, whose Merriedip prefix is still revered in the breed in this country, gave the necessary prestige and fame and popularity to the Old English. It was at this time that Mrs. Renner, then Mrs. Roesler, imported some great dogs, and the Bobtail was off and running at the U.S. dog shows. Gratitude is due her famous Pastorale and her Ch. Downderry Vanquisher, with which she won three Bests in Show!

From 1905 until 1920 Old English Sheepdog show dogs became the vogue and did a lot of winning. Some of the more famous ones were Stylish Boy, Midnight Slumber, Ch. Brentwood Hero and the two famous English imports Dolly Gray and Tip Top Weather. Several well-known exhibitors made names for themselves and their kennels at this time also. The early 1920's introduced the breeding of Mr. and Mrs. Tyler Morse of the Beaver Brook Kennels; Mr. Morris Kenney of the Kinnelong Kennels; Mr. William A. Jamison of Willinez Weather Kennels; Mrs. Joseph Urban of Yonkers; Mrs. Rumpf of Buckingham, Pennsylvania; Mrs. Laura A. Dohring of Cliffwood Kennels; Miss Edith N. Buckingham and her Cloeftaegel Kennels; Mrs. W. K. Hitchcock and Mrs. Roland M. Bakers of Woodland Farm Kennels; Mr. P. Hamilton Goodsell and son, Percy, of Tenacre Kennels; Judge and Mrs. Wilbur Kirby Hitchcock; Mrs. Doris M. Briggs of the Cartref Kennels; Fred LaCrosse and the Waltons of the Royal Kennels; Marjorie and Helen Cluff of Clearbrook; Mrs. Mary Schloss of Bovla Kennels; Mrs. V. Cline; Mrs. Rosalind Crafts of Rosmoore; many others

Edward Beegle, of Buckingham, Pennsylvania, photographed in 1923 with his Sheepdogs Pepi and Beau and Fritz (behind fence). A charming picture from the past.

also gave of their energies and time to help establish the breed during their early days in America.

The first Old English Sheepdog shown in the United States was a dog named Hempstead Bob, bred by Dr. Lock of England, and imported and owned by the Hempstead Farms. He was exhibited at the Westminster Kennel Club show in New York in 1893.

The Old English Sheepdog Club of America was founded in 1905 by Mr. Henry Arthur Tilley. After its approval by the American Kennel Club, the Old English Sheepdog Club of America held its first specialty show in 1921. This initial presentation brought out an entry of forty-two dogs. Two years

The late Hope Robinson Hitchcock with two of her fine Old English. This lady was one of many who bred top animals that paved the way for some of the great ones of modern times.

later the club's specialty show entry had gone up by only ten dogs, but the breed was, nonetheless, well on its way to a firm position in the fancy.

Mrs. George Thomas did much to popularize the breed by exhibiting at shows where Old English Sheepdogs were practically unknown and no specific classes were provided for them. Mrs. Tylor Morse also made valuable strides in the show ring by winning the Spratt's Trophy for Best Brace, All Breeds at the Garden in 1908 and 1909. She imported many of England's best Old English Sheepdogs in her efforts to help the breed establish a foothold. Mrs. Wilbur K. Hitchcock was the well-known Secretary of the Old English Sheepdog Club, starting in 1923 and for many years thereafter. P. Hamilton Goodsall, President of the club from 1919 and long after, was, in addition, a canine authority, judge, legislator and breeder of Old English. Miss E. P. Palmer

Mrs. Herbert E. Bennett of Hollywood, California, with Champion Piccadilly Circus, pictured years ago. His sire was Ch. Scallywag and his dam was Nancy Jane Scallywag.

was a past president of the club and gave valuable financial support to the club and related organizations working with the Old English Sheepdog. Dr. William Bott, a judge of Bobtails also conducted a rigorous campaign to maintain their excellence by keeping the size down and insisting on strict adherence to type and quality.

It was this guarded standard of excellence that brought several of the show dogs into prominence at this time, among them the International Champion Weather; Ch. Kennelon Halloween; Ch. Beau Brummel; Ch. Clovelly Weather; Ch. Lassie of the Farm and Ch. Montford Marksman, to name the most prominent.

From the private collection of Mr. and Mrs. Edward Beegle of Holicong, Pennsylvania comes this photo of some old-time Old English Sheepdogs, Pepi, Beau, Fritz, and their second litter of puppies. This treasured photo was taken around 1924.

A treasured photograph by Percy T. Jones of many members of the New England Old English Sheepdog Club. Left to right: Mrs. Florence A. Scannell with her Playboy Tim; Nancy G. Osgood and Pretty Please; Mr. Alonzo P. Walton, Jr., and Royal Prince Peterkin; Mrs. Walton with Ch. Royal Prince Topper; Mrs. D. Mather Briggs and Cartref Panjandrum; Mrs. Edward E. Haverstick and Cartref Hurdy Gurdy; Lois E. Foster and Button; Mrs. William L. Bailey and Sophisticated Lady; Miss Editlh N. Buckingham and Cleoftaegel Owen Elan; Mr. Fred LaCrosse and John Marksman; Mrs. William B. MacColl and Cartref Pandean; Mrs. Roland M. Baker and Woodla Minuteman; and the Rev. William L. Bailey and June.

By 1930, just a quarter of a century after the Old English Sheepdog Club had been founded in this country, the club held its Specialty in conjunction with the North Westchester Kennel Club and drew an entry of sixty-one dogs. After this show, and a reasonably large Specialty in 1931, the parent club realized that while firmly entrenched in the dog show world the tendency for the breed to gain in popularity was coming to a standstill.

Ch. Rosmoore Joy's Gift, owned, bred, and handled by the late Mrs. C.M. Crafts. Sire: Ch. Rosmoore Smarty Pants II; dam: Rosmoore Leading Lady. At the age of fifteen month this homebred was best of opposite sex at the Old English Sheepdog Club of America Specialty under judge Dr. Donald Davidson

Ch. Merriedip Master Pantaloons, owned and bred by the late Mrs. E.P. Renner, with whom he is shown. Sire: Ch. Downderry Volunteer; dam: Ch. Mistress Petticoats of Pastorale. One of the standouts in breed history, this dog brought added notice to the breed by reason of his fine show record and through his many champion children.

Ch. Bridal Gown, owned by Mrs. F. Gatehouse. Sire: Penzance Wallflower; dam: Colleen. This bitch was a prominent winner earlier in this century.

Ch. King's Messenger, owned by Stanley Kraft and bred by Julius Kraft. Sire: Ch. Merriedip of Pastorale; dam: Ch. Mistress Opal of Pastorale. This dog is another who excelled as a winner and producer.

Ch. Fernville Fernando, owned by Norman W.R. Harrison. Sire: Nero of Hardwickings; dam: Shepton Silver Wendy. This English winner finished to his championship at a very early age and has produced top winners both in Great Britain and in the United States.

Mrs. Lewis Roesler, owner of the Merriedip Kennels, at the first Bermuda dog show with her Downderry Vanquisher and Snow Bunting of Merriedip.

Mrs. Roesler and four of her Old English Sheepdogs pictured in January, 1934.

Perhaps it was this fact in itself which resulted in the parent club slowing down somewhat in their activity though various interested members in the New England area began giving added impetus to their organization, the Old English Sheepdog Club of New England. This club excelled over the parent club for two decades, until 1950 to be exact, when both clubs saw a new insurgence of members and the breed once again took a foothold up and down the eastern seaboard.

It was during the 1940's and the 1950's that the New England Club really came into its own under the guiding lights of Mrs. Crafts, Roesler, Baker and Buckingham. The Merriedip Kennels gained great fame and brought great honor to the breed with Vanquisher's three Bests In Show, and Canadian Champion Snowflake was campaigned to record wins by Marjorie and Helen Cluff of the Canadian Clearbrook Kennels. Mrs. Rosalind Crafts, in her late sixties at the time, won a Best In Show award with her Ch. Rosmoore Sinney when the dog was just fifteen months of age. And of course she scored a spectacular win, the Bobtail

The renowned Mrs. Hitchcock, of New York, and two of her famous Old English Sheepdogs of the past. Mrs. Hitchcock played an important role in the first Old English Sheepdog Club of America, and was one of its founders. This treasured photograph was loaned by Mr. and Mrs. Edward Beegle of Holicong, Pennsylvania, from their private collection of Bobtails and their owners from the first half of this century.

The Grindstone of Pastorale, owned by George G. Frelinghuysen Jr. and handled by Walter Morris, wins the Best In Show award at the April 14, 1940 Union County Kennel Club show. Mr. A. Clinton Wilmerding was the judge, with Mr. John L. Mulson presenting the trophy. Photograph by Percy T. Jones.

Champion Mistress Merrie O'Merriedip, the Old English which won Best of Breed at the 1940 Morris and Essex Kennel Club show. Owned by Mrs. Alonzo P. Walton, Jr., Mistress Merrie was shown 14 times and captured seven Bests of Breed, a Group First and five group placings. She was either Best of Breed or Best of Opposite Sex each time she was shown in 1940.

Best In Show win at Morris and Essex in 1938, with Ch. Ideal Weather!

Dog shows were greatly curtailed during the early 1940's because of World War II gas rationing, but the devoted Bobtail breeders managed to persevere, and Mrs. Renner went on campaigning and winning at the shows with the renowned Ch. Merriedip Mister Pantaloons, Ch. Merriedip Mr. Personality, Ch. King's Messenger, Ch. Black Baron and Ch. Royal Victor, among others.

Handler Alf Loveridge with Ch. Ideal Weather, Best In Show dog at the 1938 Morris and Essex Kennel Club show in New Jersey. The classic "M & E" event was always considered "the prestige show" among the fanciers, since it was one of the most beautifully staged dog shows in the United States. The show was held on the grounds of the Horace Dodge estate and was master-minded by Mrs. Horace M. Dodge, whose Giralda dogs were also world-famous. Photo by William Brown.

Ch. Merriedip of Pastorale, owned by Mrs. Helen Margery Lewis, captured a Best In Show at the Westbury Kennel Association several years ago. The judge was Harry T. Peters. Mrs. William H. Long, President of the Club, presents the trophy, with Mrs. Lewis handling. Photo by William Brown.

The well-known Best In Show Old English Rosmoore Simrey, pictured here winning under Mrs. Geraldine R. Dodge at the Framingham District Kennel Club in Massachusetts on June 1, 1958. Club President Kenneth C. Tiffin also presents a trophy to Simrey and his owner-handler, Mrs. Rosalind Crafts. Photo by Evelyn Shafer.

Best American Bred Dog In Show, Ch. Rosmoore Saint John, owned by Mrs. Helen M. Lewis, who handled her dog to the top of this 39th Annual dog show of the Ladies Kennel Association of America held at Garden City, New York on Saturday, May 16, 1942. The judge was Charles P. Scott; club president Mrs. H. H. Neal is pictured at center in this Percy T. Jones photograph.

BEST
AMERICAN BRED
IN SHOW

BEST DOG
IN
SHOW

Westminster 1942 found the winner of the Working Group the Old English Sheepdog Ch. Merriedip Master Pantaloons, then owned by Mrs. Helen M. Lewis; the handler was George McKercher.

Best in the Working Dog Group at the Westchester Kennel Club Show in September, 1958 was Mrs. Marvin Kucker's Ch. Merriedip Duke George. Here the judge is the late respected Albert E. Van Court. Mrs. Kucker, now Mrs. Mona Berkowitz, handles her dog.

After the Second World War, perhaps the greatest dog in the breed to date, Ch. Merriedip Duke George, emerged from Mrs. Renner's famous kennel . . . owned and handled by Mrs. Mona Kucker Berkowitz. George was perhaps the most famous of all Bobtails during the 1950's and was followed by the great showdog and sire, Ch. Fezziwig Ceiling Zero, owned by the Hendrik Van

Rensselaers. This magnificent dog won fifteen Bests In Show. Around this time we were seeing winning in the rings by a lovely Canadian dog, Ch. Blue Admiral of Box. Other United States winners were Ch. Shepton Surprise; Ch. Tarawoods Blue Baron, winner of nine Bests in Show; and Ch. B. and H's Holiday Showcase . . . all strong contenders in the show rings and on the rating charts.

In 1964 Ch. Fezziwig Raggedy Andy set records with thirteen Bests in Show and ranked second of all Working Dogs that year according to *Popular Dogs* magazine's famous Phillips System ratings of the top show dogs in the nation. Ch. Tarawood's Blue Baron ranked third right below him. In 1965 Ch. Fezziwig

Ch. Tarawood's Blue Baron wins Best In Show at the Ft. Lauderdale Dog Show in January, 1964, with Charles Meyer handling. The judge was Mr. Cyrus Rickel. Baron is owned by Adeline H. Isakson. An Alexander photo.

American and Canadian Champion Tamara's Shaggy Shoes MacDuff, Best In Show winner owner/handled by Don McColl, who co-owns "Duffy" with his wife, Jean. Now retired at stud, Duffy's record at the termination of his show ring career was 78 Bests of Breed, 31 Group placements, one of the Top Ten Old English Sheepdogs for two years in a row and No. 2 Sheepdog in Canada for two years as well. Photo by Martin Booth.

Ch. Momarv's Mighty Like a Rose, Sire: Ch. Shayloran's Billy Hayseed; dam: Momarv's Burning Bright. This handsome youngster, line-bred on the immortal Ch. Merriedip Duke, has already proven to be a worthy winner.

American and Canadian Champion Blue Admiral of Box, an English import, taking Best In Show in 1963. He sired many champions, including the first litter of Old English Sheepdogs at the Beau Cheval Kennels of the Andersons in Wycombe, Pennsylvania.

May 1968

Special
WORKING GROUP
ISSUE

50 cents

The May, 1968 cover of *Popular Dogs* magazine featured this marvelous picture of the Howard B. Paynes' great winning Old English Sheepdog Ch. Rivermist Dan Patch sharing an intimate moment with his handler, Jack Funk. At the time this cover appeared Dan Patch was America's top-winning Bobtail. Photo by Ritter.

Ch. Prince Andrew of Sherline pictured taking one of his many wins, this one under judge William Kendrick. Andrew won the distinction of being one of the breed's all-time top winning Bobtails. In 1969 he was not only the number one Old English Sheepdog in the nation according to the *Popular Dogs* magazine's Phillips System ratings but also was number one Working Dog in the nation and number three of all breeds! Andrew was handled throughout his career by Robert Forsyth for owners Mr. and Mrs. Howard Sherline of Detroit, Michigan. Andrew also was number one Old English in 1970 and 1971; in 1970 he was number three among the Working Breeds and in 1971 number two among the Working Breeds.

Raggedy Andy was back to top his 1964 record by being top Old English Sheepdog in the country and fifth ranking dog of all breeds in the nation. In 1966 he ranked #1!

Champion Prince Andrew of Sherline was warming up in the bull pen around this time and later came into prominence as top Old English Sheepdog, breaking records. Ch. Rivermist Hollyhock, sired by the Barry Goodmans' magnificent import, International Champion Unesta Pim, became one of the few undefeated Bobtail bitches in the show ring. Mona Berkowitz

Photographed in October, 1965 was Barry Goodman's remarkable import, Bahlambs Unnesta Pim, which he campaigned to one of the nation's top winning—and top-producing—Old English Sheepdogs. Mr. Goodman is the owner of the famous Rivermist Kennels, Bethesda, Maryland. Photo by Evelyn M. Shafer.

introduced from her famous Mornarv Kennels many top contenders for the winner's circle. And today Mona Berkowitz, the Van Rensselaers and Barry Goodman are still among the top ranking names in breed ranks.

Other of today's leading kennel prefixes are Morrows, Bear Creak, Knightcap, Windfield, Droverdale, Silvershag, Beau Cheval, Ticklebee, Sunnybrae, St. Trinian, Bahlambs, Silvermist,

American and Canadian Champion Rivermist Dan Tatters, pictured winning the First in the Working Group under James Trullinger at the 1969 Canadian National Sportsmen's Show. Co-owned by Mr. and Mrs. O. R. Ziccardi and his handler, James McTernan, Dan Tatters was top Producing Sire of 1971 with eight Champion get for the year. He is at the present time No. 3 Top Producer of all time in the breed with a total of 20 Champion offspring to his credit. Tatters was whelped September 9, 1965.

International Champion Ragbears Lady of Agincourt is pictured winning a Group First in Mexico City in December, 1971. Lady is a champion in Canada, Mexico and the United States. The judge is Isadore Schoenberg. Lady is co-owned by her breeder, Gail Fletcher of Tucson, Arizona and Alex and Lillian Gross of Poulsbo, Washington.

A marvelous mother-daughter photograph taken at the Rivermist Kennels of Barry Goodman in Bethesda, Maryland.

Tamara, Greyfriar, Waterfall, Ambelon, Double J, Tatters, Happytown, Ivyridge, Tarawoods, Jendowers, Robinswood, Bufferton, Shaggybar, Rosecliffs, Misty Isles, Beaverbrooks, Loyalblue, Windswept, Shiler, Gigglewyck, Windjammer, Downeyland, Echoe Valley, Lillibrad, Crofton, Orchards, Ragbear, Bobmar, and many others.

All who wish to pursue the showing, raising, breeding or owning of a Bobtail must join a club where complete records and advice can be given to prospective owners and members. The latest information on active clubs in your area or informatjon on the Old English Sheepdog in general can be obtained by contacting the Old English Sheepdog Club of America directly, or through the American Kennel Club.

CHAPTER 3

AMERICAN KENNEL CLUB STANDARD FOR THE BREED

(American Kennel Club, Approved October 13, 1953*)*

SKULL—Capacious and rather squarely formed, giving plenty of room for brain power. The parts over the eyes should be well arched and the whole well covered with hair.

JAW—Fairly long, strong, square and truncated. The top should be well defined to avoid a Deerhound face. (The attention of judges is particularly called to the above properties, as a long, narrow head is a deformity.)

EYES—Vary according to the color of the dog. Very dark preferred, but in the glaucous or blue dogs a pearl, walleye or china eye is considered typical. (A light eye is most objectionable.)

NOSE—Always black, large and capacious.

TEETH—Strong and large, evenly placed and level in opposition.

EARS—Medium-sized, and carried flat to side of head, coated moderately.

LEGS—The forelegs should be dead straight, with plenty of bone, removing the body a medium height from the ground, without approaching legginess, and well coated all around.

FEET—Small, round; toes well arched, and pads thick and hard.

TAIL—It is preferable that there should be none. Should never, however, exceed 1½ or 2 inches in grown dogs. When not natural-born bobtails however, puppies should be docked at the first joint from the body and the operation performed when they are from three to four days old.

NECK AND SHOULDERS—The neck should be fairly long, arched gracefully and well coated with hair. The shoulders sloping and narrow at the points, the dog standing lower at the shoulder than at the loin.

BODY—Rather short and very compact, ribs well sprung and brisket deep and capacious. *Slabsidedness highly undesirable.* The loin should be very stout and gently arched, while the hindquarters

Mrs. Joseph Urban with two of her Old English, Pepi and his son, photographed in the garden of her Yonkers, New York home. This treasured photograph supplied by Mr. Edward Beegle, of Buckingham, Pennsylvania.

should be round and muscular and with well-let-down hocks, and the hams densely coated with a thick, long jacket in excess of any other part.

COAT—Profuse, but not so excessive as to give the impression of the dog being overfat, and of a good hard texture; not straight, but shaggy and free from curl. *Quality and texture of coat to be considered above mere profuseness.* Softness or flatness or coat to be considered a fault. The undercoat should be a waterproof pile, when not removed by grooming or season.

An Old English which has been shaved down to the skin presents the true picture of Old English Sheepdog conformation.

An "off guard" moment with Mrs. Hitchcock and one of her Old English Sheepdogs choosing this moment to roll over and play dead for the camera!

COLOR—Any shade of gray, grizzle, blue or blue-merled with or without white markings or in reverse. *Any shade of brown or fawn to be considered distinctly objectionable and not to be encouraged.*

SIZE—Twenty-two inches and upwards for dogs and slightly less for bitches. Type, character and symmetry are of the greatest importance and are on no account to be sacrified to size alone.

GENERAL APPEARANCE AND CHARACTERISTICS—A strong, compact-looking dog of great symmetry, practically the same in measureemnt from shoulder to stern as in height, absolutely free from legginess or weaselness, very elastic in his gallop, but in walking or trotting he has a characteristic ambling or pacing movement, and his bark should be loud, with a peculiar "pot-casse" ring in it. Taking him all round, he is a profusely, but not *excessively* coated, thick-set, muscular, able-bodied dog with a most intelligent expression, free from all Poodle or Deerhound character. *Soundness should be considered of greatest importance.*

Scale of Points

Skull	5
Eyes	5
Ears	5
Teeth	5
Nose	5
Jaw	5
Foreface	5
Neck and shoulders	5
Body and loins	10
Hindquarters	10
Legs	10
Coat (texture, quality and condition)	15
General appearance and movement	15
Total	100

CHAPTER 4

BUYING YOUR OLD ENGLISH SHEEPDOG PUPPY

There are several trails that will lead you to a litter of puppies where you can find the puppy of your choice. Write to the parent club and ask for the names and addresses of members who have puppies for sale. The addresses of your breed's clubs can be secured by writing the American Kennel Club, 51 Madison Avenue, New York, N.Y. 10010. They keep an accurate, up-to-date list of reputable breeders where you can seek information on obtaining a good, healthy puppy. You might also check listings in the classified ads of major newspapers. The various dog magazines also carry listings; for example, Popular Dogs magazine carries a column on the breed each and every month.

It is to your advantage to attend a few dog shows in the area where thoroughbred dogs of just about every breed are being exhibited in the show ring. Even if you do not wish to buy a show dog, you should be familiar with what the better specimens look like so that you may at least get a worthy specimen for your money. You will learn a lot by observing the dogs in action in the show ring, or in a public place where their personalities come to the fore. The dog show catalogue will list the dogs and their owners with local kennel names and breeders which you can visit to see the types they are breeding and winning with at the shows. Exhibitors at these shows are usually delighted to talk to people about their dogs and the specific characteristics of this particular breed.

Once you have chosen the dog of your choice from all the breeds because you admire its exceptional beauty, intelligence and personality, and because you feel the breed will fit in with your family's way of life, it is wise to do a little research on the breed.

Typical puppy head study of the Old English Sheepdog. Beau Cheval's Short Notice, owned by Charles L. Marciante, of Pennington, New Jersey.

The American Kennel Club library, your local library, bookshops, and the club can usually supply you with a list of reading matter or written material on the breed, past and present. Then once you have drenched yourself in the breed's illustrious history and have definitely decided that this is the dog for you, it is time to start writing letters and making phone calls to set up appointments to see litters of puppies!

A word of caution here: don't let your choice of a kennel be determined by its nearness to your home, and then buy the first "cute" puppy that races up to you or licks the end of your nose! All puppies are cute, and naturally you will have a preference among those you see. But don't let preferences sway you into making a wrong decision.

If you are buying your dog as a family pet, a preference might not be a serious offense. But if you have had, say, a color preference since you first considered this breed, you would be wise to stick to it—color or coat pattern is important because you will want your dog to be pleasing to the eye as well. And if you are buying a show dog, an accepted coat or color pattern is essential, according to the Standard for the breed. In considering your purchase you must think clearly, choose carefully, and make the very best possible choice. You will, of course, learn to love your puppy which ever one you finally decide upon, but a case of "love at first sight" can be disappointing and expensive later on, if a show career was your primary objective.

To get the broadest possible concept of what is for sale and the current market prices, it is recommended that you visit as many kennels and private breeders as possible. With today's reasonably safe, inexpensive and rapid flights on the major airlines, it is possible to secure dogs from far-off places at nominal additional charges, which will allow you to buy the valuable bloodline of your choice, if you have a thought toward a breeding program in the future.

While it is always safest to actually *see* the dog you are buying, there are enough reputable breeders and kennels to be found for you to buy a dog with a minimum of risk once you have made up your mind what you want, and when you have decided whether you will buy in this country or import to satisfy your concept of the breed Standard. If you are going to breed dogs, breeding Standard

An adorable little puppy bitch named Panda Bear, owned by Mrs. Edye Weinberg of Baltimore, Maryland.

type is a moral obligation, and your concern should be with buying the very best bloodlines and individual animals obtainable, in spite of cost or distance.

It is customary for the purchaser to pay the shipping charges, and the airlines are most willing to supply flight information and prices upon request. Rental on the shipping crate, if the owner does not provide one for the dog, is nominal. While unfortunate instances have occurred on the airlines in the transporting of animals by air, the major airlines are making improvements on safety measures and have reached the point of reasonable safety and cost. Barring unforeseen circumstances, the safe arrival of a dog you might buy can pretty much be assured if both seller and purchaser adhere to and follow up on even the most minute details from both ends.

THE PUPPY YOU BUY

Let us assume you want to enjoy all the antics of a young puppy and decide to buy a six- to eight-week-old puppy. This is about the age when a puppy is weaned, wormed and ready to go out into the world with a responsible new owner. It is better not to buy a puppy under six weeks of age, they simply are not yet ready to leave the mother. At eight to twelve weeks of age you will be able to notice much about the appearance and the behavior. Puppies, as they are remembered in our fondest childhood memories, are gay and active and bouncy, as well they should be! The normal puppy should be interested, alert, and curious, especially about a stranger. If a puppy acts a little reserved or distant, however, this need not be misconstrued as shyness or fear. It merely indicates he hasn't made up his mind if he likes you as yet! By the same token, he should not be fearful or terrified by a stranger—and especially should not show any fear of his owner!

In direct contrast, the puppy should not be ridiculously overactive either. The puppy that frantically bounds around the room and is never still is not particularly desirable. And beware of "spinners!" Spinners are the puppies or dogs that have become neurotic from being kept in cramped quarters or in crates and behave in this emotionally unstable manner when loosed in adequate space. When released they run in circles and seemingly "go wild." Puppies with this kind of traumatic background seldom ever regain full composure or adjust to the big outside world. The puppy which has had the proper exercise and appropriate living quarters will have a normal, though spirited, outlook on life and will do his utmost to win you over without having to go into a tailspin.

If the general behavior and appearance of the dog thus far appeals to you, it is time for you to observe him more closely for additional physical requirements. First of all, you cannot expect to find in the puppy all the coat he will bear upon maturity, thanks to good food and the many wonderful grooming aids which can be found on the market today. Needless to say, the healthy puppy's coat should have a nice shine to it, and the more dense at this age, the better the coat will be when the dog reaches adulthood.

Look for clear, dark, sparkling eyes, free of discharge. Dark eye rims and lids are indications of good pigmentation which is important in a breeding program, or even for generally pleasing good looks. From the time the puppy first opens his eyes until he is about three months old, however, it must be remembered that the eyes have a slight blue-ish cast to them. The older the puppy, the darker the eye, so always ascertain the age of the puppy and the degree of darkness that should be in the eye at this particular time of its life.

Typical shaggy dog expression on this typical Old English Sheepdog puppy owned by Charles L. Marciante. Dog's official name is Beau Cheval's Short Notice.

When the time comes to select your puppy, take an experienced breeder along with you. If this is not possible, take the Standard for the breed with you. These Standards may be obtained from the local club or found in the *American Kennel Club Dog Book* which can be obtained at any library. Then try to interpret the Standard as best you can by making comparisons between the puppies you see.

Check the bite completely and carefully. While the first set of teeth can be misleading, even the placement of teeth at this young age can be a fairly accurate indication of what the bite will be in the grown dog. The gums should be a good healthy pink in color, and the teeth should be clear, clean and white. Any brown cast to them could mean a past case of distemper, and would assuredly count against the dog in the show ring, or against the dog's general appearance at maturity:

Puppies take anything and everything into their mouths to chew on while they are teething, and a lot of infectious diseases are introduced this way. The aforementioned distemper is one, and the brown teeth as a result of this disease never clear. The puppy's breath should not be sour or even unpleasant or strong. Any acrid odor could indicate a poor mixture of food, or low quality of meat, especially if it is being fed raw. Many breeders have compared the

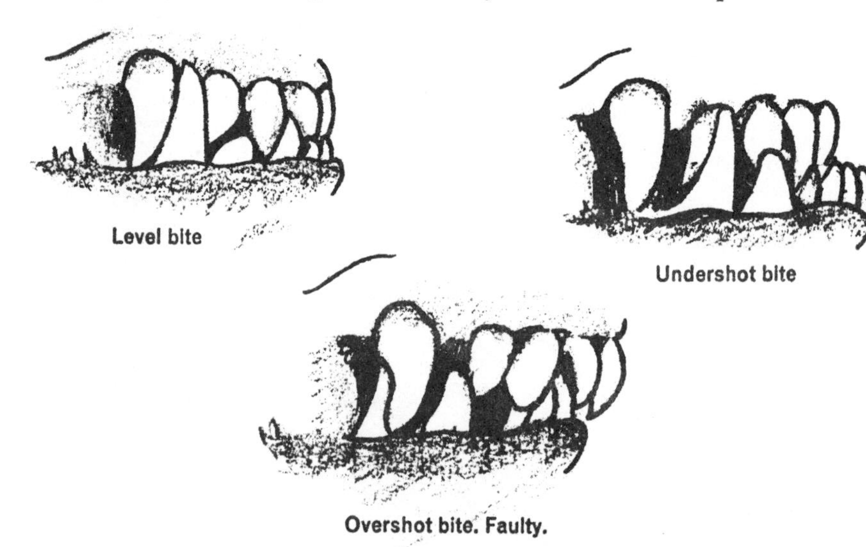
Level bite

Undershot bite

Overshot bite. Faulty.

Champion Beau Cheval's Lord Little Chap, bred by Marlene J. Anderson and pictured with his owners, the Demateis sisters of New Brunswick, New Jersey.

breath of a healthy puppy to that of fresh toast, or as being vaguely like garlic. At any rate, a puppy should never be fed just table scraps, but should have a well-balanced diet containing a good dry puppy chow, and a good grade of fresh meat. Poor meat, too much cereal, or fillers, tend to make the puppy too fat. We like puppies to be in good flesh, but not fat from the wrong kind of food!

It goes without saying that we want to find clean puppies. The breeder or owner who shows you a dirty puppy is one from whom to steer away! Look closely at the skin. Rub the fur the wrong way or against the grain; make sure it is not spotted with insect bites, or red, blotchy sores or dry scales. The vent area around the tail should not show evidences of diarrhea or inflammation. By the same token, the puppy's fur should not be matted with dry excrement or smell of urine.

True enough, you can wipe dirty eyes, clean dirty ears, and give the puppy a bath when you get it home, but these are all indications of how the puppy has been cared for during the important formative first months of its life, and can vitally influence its future health and development. There are many reputable breeders raising healthy puppies that have been reared in proper places and under the proper conditions in clean establishments, so why take a chance on a series of veterinary bills and a questionable constitution?

MALE OR FEMALE?

The choice of sex in your puppy is also something that must be given serious thought before you shop. Here again, for the pet owner, the sex that would best suit the family life you enjoy would be the paramount choice to consider. For the breeder or exhibitor, there are other considerations. If you are looking for a stud to establish a kennel, it is essential that you select a dog with both testicles evident, even at a tender age, and verified by a veterinarian before the sale is finalized.

One testicle, or a monorchid, automatically disqualifies the dog from the show ring or from a breeding program, though monorchids are capable of siring. Additionally, it must be noted that monorchids frequently sire dogs with the same deficiency, and to introduce this into a bloodline knowingly is an unwritten sin in the dog fancy. Also, a monorchid can sire cryptorchids. Cryptorchids have no testicles and are sterile.

If you desire a dog to be a member of the family, the best selection would probably be a female. You can always go out for

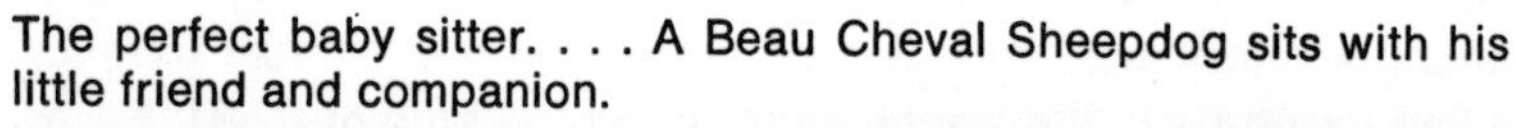

The perfect baby sitter. . . . A Beau Cheval Sheepdog sits with his little friend and companion.

stud service if you should decide to breed. You can choose the bloodlines doing the most winning because they should be bred true to type, and you will not have to foot the bill for the financing of a show career. You can always keep a male from your first litter that will bear your own "kennel name" if you have decided to proceed in the "kennel business."

An additional consideration in the male versus female decision for the private owner is that with males, there might be the problem of leg-lifting and with females, there is the inconvenience while they are in season. However, this need not be the problem it used to be—pet shops sell "pants" for both sexes, which help to control this situation in the home.

THE PLANNED PARENTHOOD BEHIND YOUR PUPPY

Never be afraid to ask pertinent questions about the puppy, as well as questions about the sire and dam. Feel free to ask the breeder if you might see the dam, not only to establish her general health, but her appearance as a representative of the breed. Ask also to see the sire if they are his owners. Ask what the puppy has been fed and should be fed after weaning. Ask to see the pedigree, and inquire if the litter or the individual puppies have been registered with the American Kennel Club, how many of the temporary and/or permanent inoculations the puppy has had, when and if the puppy has been wormed, and if it has had any illness, disease or infection.

You need not ask if the puppy is housebroken . . . it won't mean much. He may have gotten the idea as to where "the place" is where he now lives, but he will need new training to learn where "the place" is in his new home! And you can't really expect too much from them at this age anyway. Housebreaking is entirely up to the new owner. We know puppies always eliminate after they eat, so it is up to you to remember to take the dog out immediately after each meal. They also eliminate when they first awaken and sometimes dribble when they get excited. If friends and relatives are coming over to see the new puppy, make sure he is walked before he greets them at the front door. This will help.

The normal time period for puppies around three months of age to eliminate is about two to three hours. So as the time draws near, either take the puppy out or indicate the newspapers for the same purpose. Housebreaking is never easy, but anticipation is about 90 per cent of the problem. The schools that offer to housebreak your dog are virtually useless. Here again the puppy will learn the "place" at the schoolhouse, but coming home he will need new training for the new location.

A reputable breeder will welcome any and all questions you might ask and will voluntarily offer additional information, if only to brag about the tedious and loving care he has given his litter. He will also sell a puppy on 24 hour veterinary approval. This means you have a full day to get the puppy to a veterinarian of your choice to get his opinion on the general health of the puppy before you make a final decision. There should also be veterinary certificates and full particulars on the dates and types of inoculations the puppy has been given to date.

PUPPIES AND WORMS

Let us give further attention to the unhappy and very unpleasant subject of worms. Generally speaking, most all puppies—even those raised in clean quarters—come into contact with worms early in life. They can be passed down from the mother before birth or picked up during their first encounters with the earth or quarters. To say that you must not buy a puppy because of the presence of worms is nonsensical. You might be passing up a fine

Beau Chevals Muffin, pictured at six weeks of age. Muffin now lives with her owners in California.

quality animal that can be freed of worms in one short treatment. True, a heavy infestation of worms of any kind in a young dog is dangerous and debilitating.

The extent of infection can be readily determined by a veterinarian and you might take his word as to whether the future health and conformation of the dog has been damaged. He can prescribe the dosage and supply the medication at the time and you will already have one of your problems solved. The kinds and varieties of worms and how to detect them is described in detail elsewhere in this book and we advise you to check the matter out further if there is any doubt in your mind as to the problems of worms in dogs.

Young Master Roeder of Mechanicsville, Pennsylvania, with his friend and companion, Beau Cheval's Honey Fitz.

VETERINARY INSPECTION

While your veterinarian is going over the puppy you have selected to purchase, you might just as well ask him for his opinion of it as a breed of dog as well as facts about its general health. While few veterinarians can claim to be breed standard experts, they

Siesta time! Little Melinda Jordan catches forty winks with Ch. Taralane's Beauregard Bleu, CD, a homebred champion owned by Dr. and Mrs. Hugh Jordan of Whittier, California.

usually have a "good eye" for a fine specimen and can advise you where to go for further information. Perhaps they can also recommend other breeders for opinions. The vet can point out structural faults or organic problems that affect all breeds and can usually judge whether an animal has been abused or mishandled and whether it is over- or undersized.

We would like to emphasize here that it is only through this type of close cooperation between owners and veterinarians that we can expect to reap the harvest of modern research and advance. Most reputable veterinarians are more than eager to learn about various purebred dogs, and we in turn must acknowledge and apply what they have proven through experience and research in their field. We can buy and breed the best dog in the world, but when disease strikes we are only as safe as our veterinarian is capable—so let us keep them informed breed by breed and dog by dog! The veterinarian represents the difference between life and death!

CHAPTER 5

HOW TO SELECT THE BEST OLD ENGLISH SHEEPDOG PUPPY

THE TEMPERAMENT OF THE OLD ENGLISH SHEEPDOG

No matter what his intended purpose on earth, the Old English Sheepdog is basically a clown! He is funloving and obedient, and although he is an excellent watchdog, he is friendly with anyone you accept into your home, with few exceptions.

Sometimes our dogs know more about people than we do, and for some reason unknown to us, our Sheepdog may never accept certain people (children included) or certain other animals. But this should be an exception rather than a rule, and, generally speaking, can apply to most breeds.

The Old English is at his best when given complete freedom. We do not believe that they are at their best in kennels, but rather excel as house dogs when they are accepted by everyone and made a member of the family. The ideal environment of course is their natural one, in the fields or on farms giving vent to their energy and serving as working dogs. But this is almost a lost cause for today's Sheepdogs. They are destined to become either house dogs or kennel dogs and, in too many instances, small-apartment house dogs! Big cities are overrun with the big shaggy dogs that everyone loves but few are able to keep and groom properly.

In the city it is next to impossible to keep Old English Sheepdogs as clean as they should be, and the limited living space means frustrations for the dog. They are almost certain to become ill-tempered, unpredictable, fearbiters or "psycho." Then unknowing

Something new to chew! Mik Ron Photographers captured this beautiful likeness of the Old English Sheepdog owned by Barbara Diehl of Santa Clara, California.

owners have them destroyed because they believe them to be dangerous, when ironically enough, they themselves made them that way.

A spacious house with large backyard, or a kennel with large exercise yards is ideal, but also allow for time indoors with the family. And the same rules should apply to the puppies. Even those which will grow up to be kennel dogs should still spend time in the house with the family. This is essential if the puppies are to go from a kennel into a private home.

Crates are taboo where the Bobtails are concerned. They are simply not suited for them. A dog which is meant to course the fields should never spend time in wall-to-wall confinement. The dog which is properly trained and socialized will not be so wild or exuberant that he will have to be crated when company comes or when not outdoors.

This socializing is a most important part of early training. The dog should be handled only by people and children who have been taught the *proper* way to handle a puppy. The Sheepdog puppy may never forget the hard bang on the head from a little child or being carried around by a leg or dragged by the ear. This could result in the dog's mistrusting and disliking children the rest of its life.

A Sheepdog's world should extend beyond its own home and kennel yard also. From the time the puppy is safely immunized it should be taken along with the family in the car for rides, to the supermarket and on visits to the homes of other dog lovers. This will not only serve to socialize the puppy but will help immeasurably if you intend to show the dog.

Sheepdogs are a lot like horses . . . they get their "horse sense" when they are around two years old. This is one reason it is advisable to wait until this age, or a little longer, before you breed the bitches. They are better able to cope with the requirements of motherhood when they are past young maidenhood.

In our desire to produce long hair and short bodies and win the blue ribbons, we have overlooked one of the most important qualities of our Sheepdogs. *Good temperament* should be outlined in the Standard—and it isn't!

If you plan to buy or breed your first Old English Sheepdog we feel it is very important to look into the background of the parents;

Champion Tamara's Patches of Perse gets into the legitimate theater appearing with movie and stage star Patricia Morrison in *Camelot.* Patches is owned by Tammy and Marvin Smith, Tamara Kennels, Brighton, Michigan.

it is better still to visit them and see them in person. Puppies which bite at your ankles or shoelaces, or tug on trouser legs are not vicious, as some novice dog owners think. This is normal behavior. But the four-month old puppy that bites the judge when he examines his teeth or bites the owner when he tries to take the feed pan is something else again. It can be an indication of serious trouble.

Dogs can lose their minds and go insane just as some people do. If something seems to be wrong, look into it right away before it ends in serious injury to someone . . . and more than likely to a child. A large, mean dog, of any breed, is dangerous. Avoid it and do NOT use such a dog for breeding.

Remember that today some owners breed dogs not just for fun or perfection, but for profit, too, so they aren't all necessarily what we would like them to be. Man is the culprit . . . not the dog.

Most breeds are suffering from too much popularity and overbreeding. When you find a certain breed on every block or in every pet store in almost every town you know this to be tragic and true. Therefore, everyone has to be even more selective in choosing a pet for breeding or show stock.

The Old English Sheepdog is a great dog for the entire family because he is, as we said before, a real clown!

SPECIAL PUPPY TRAITS TO LOOK FOR

Once you have evaluated all the general problems that a new puppy poses, and once you have decided that you are contemplating purchasing this puppy from the very best possible source, you are ready to get down to the finer points for your selection. If you are not able to take along an experienced and knowledgeable breeder or owner who has purchased a puppy which turned out well in the past, the final decision you make must be based on something more substantial than a whim.

Co-author Marlene Anderson poses with two three-week-old Bobtail puppies at her Beau Cheval Farms in Wycombe, Pennsylvania.

With the Old English Sheepdog you must not go on markings alone! That white-headed puppy with two brown eyes and dark eye rims may have very little else to offer when matched against the Standard. The Old English puppy should give the impression of having a square body. He should have heavy bones and straight legs well under him. With this over-all picture in mind, narrow your selection down to just two . . . or you will become confused and will fall in love with each one of them all over again. Ask to keep just these two puppies on view and watch them run around and play for a while. Take this opportunity to notice which is widest in the front and rear and the soundest in both body and mind . . . in other words, don't overlook the showmanship and the outgoing personality characteristic of the Old English Sheepdog. Don't be overly impressed by the puppies that just play . . . look for the one that plays but is alert to outside sounds and people. This might mean that the genes for the companion and guard dog are present.

THE CONDITIONS OF SALE

While it is customary to pay for the puppy before you take it away with you, you should be able to give the breeder a deposit, if there is any doubt about the puppy's health. You might also postdate a check to cover the 24-hour veterinary approval. If you do decide to take the puppy the breeder is required to supply you with a pedigree, along with the puppy's registration paper. He is also obliged to supply you with complete information and American Kennel Club instructions on how to transfer ownership of the puppy into your name.

Some breeders will offer buyers time payment plans for convenience, if the price on a show dog is very high, or if deferred payments are the only possible way you can purchase the dog. However, any such terms must be worked out between buyer and breeder and should be put in writing to avoid later complications.

You will find most breeders cooperative if they believe you are sincere in your love for the puppy and that you will give it the proper home and show ring career, if it is sold as a show quality specimen of the breed. Remember, when buying a show dog, it is impossible to guarantee nature. A breeder can only tell you what

Before leaving to join her new owners in California, the six-year-old Champion Beau Chevals Perri-Winkle poses with friend Julie Howard to see who is coming up to the fence. Perri-Winkle was bred and originally owned by Marlene J. Anderson, of Wycombe, Pennsylvania.

he *believes* will develop into a show quality dog. So be sure your breeder is an honest one.

Also, it is only fair to the breeder that if you purchase a show specimen and promise to show the dog, that you do show it! It is a waste to have a beautiful dog that deserves recognition in the show ring sitting at home as a family pet. This is especially true if the breeder offered you a reduced price because of the advertising his kennel and bloodlines would receive by your showing the dog in the ring. If you want a pet, buy a pet. Be honest about it, and let the breeder decide on this basis which is the best dog for you. Your conscience will be clear and you'll both be doing a real service to the breed.

BUYING AND BREEDING SHOW PUPPIES

If you plan to breed or show your puppy, make it clear that you intend to do so, so that the breeder will help you select the very best puppy. If you are dealing with a reputable breeder and an established kennel, you must rely partially if not entirely on their choice, since they know their bloodlines and what they can produce better than anyone else. He knows how his stock develops, and he would be foolish to sell you a puppy that could not stand up as a breed force or that would misrepresent his stock in the show ring.

However, you must also realize that the breeder may be keeping the best puppy in the litter to show and breed himself. If this is the case, you might be wise to select the best puppy of the opposite sex so that the dogs will not be competing against one another in the show rings for their championship points.

Prices vary on all puppies, of course, but a good show prospect at eight weeks to six months of age will sell for several hundred dollars. If the puppy is outstanding, and the pedigree and parentage the same, it will go higher. Reputable breeders, however, stand behind their puppies and should something drastic develop, such as Hip Dysplasia, etc., their obligation to make an adjustment is usually honored.

COST OF BUYING YOUNG ADULTS OR GROWN STOCK

Prices in this category really fluctuate. Some grown dogs are offered free of charge, or are put out with owners on breeder's terms. But do not count on obtaining a worthy dog free of charge. Good dogs are much in demand. Most of the worthy brood bitches are quite expensive. For a valuable show and breeding specimen over one year of age, of either sex, you must be prepared to pay somewhere around $1,000. Dogs of this calibre are difficult to find and do not come cheap, as many wealthy people have found out!

CHAPTER 6

OLD ENGLISH SHEEPDOGS AND THEIR SPECIAL CHARACTERISTICS

COLORING ON OLD ENGLISH SHEEPDOGS

Our Standard calls for any shade of gray, grizzle, blue or blue-merled with or without white markings or in reverse. This should leave little room for error in identifying a mismarked Old English Sheepdog. Although some frown on Sheepdogs with white patches on their bodies, a patch an inch or two in size should not panic a breeder if the dog is otherwise typey. For instance, a bitch with a patch of white the size of a sheet of typing paper on a gray back might never reproduce such a marking if she's bred.

Any shade of brown or fawn color is considered distinctly objectionable and is not to be encouraged, though a few such dogs are seen. To keep the coat its purest blue or blue gray, living quarters where sunshine is prevalent should be avoided. Covered runs are an absolute must.

With few exceptions, Sheepdogs are born black and white. The black begins to turn silvery at about twelve weeks of age, though it might happen later in certain bloodlines. This silvering will gradually creep up the hocks and into the rest of the coat. If you examine the coat carefully, you will see a gray undercoat coming in on the "teenage" puppies. A Sheepdog which remains black and white and never turns to a lighter gray is definitely "wrong"! But the true puppy will gradually turn blue, silver and gray with age.

No matter what poetic name you give to the color of your Sheep-dog—and we've heard terms such as *sea-foam blue, silver white,*

Two male Old English Sheepdog puppies born January 10, 1972 and pictured at eight weeks of age. Puppy on the left has white head except for black on right ear, which will turn silver gray and will blend in, making the puppy appear to be all white-headed at maturity. Bred by Marlene Anderson, these puppies were sired by Beau Cheval Ibsen ex Orphan Annie.

slate gray and *pewter blue, pigeon's egg blue* seems to be the favourite! And since the beauty is in the eye of the beholder, we can only suggest that you look for good contrast between the blue and the white. The silver white or a silver which is so light that both colors pale, or the markedly black and white dog, should be avoided, especially if you intend to breed. We must note here, however, that one of Europe and America's biggest winners was nearly all gray, with very little white.

The misconception that a Sheepdog is better because it exhibits a white head is all wrong, and those that seek white-headed puppies, overlooking all the rest of the qualities, are mistaken. Many believe these are what the judges prefer, but it simply is not so! New breeders who price their white-headed puppies higher than the rest, or sell them as special showdogs, are as ignorant as those buyers who seek them.

Black eye rims are also of great concern to many breeders and buyers, and *some* judges! True, they are impressive on a Sheepdog, and certainly we would prefer black rims in preference to the pink pigment, but black eye rims are not necessarily the mark of the best dog. Too many judges make this a deciding factor between the dog that wins and the dog that loses. Only when all other things are equal should eye rim color be the deciding factor.

In puppies with black masks the black pigmentation is there already, but that is not always the case for their white-headed littermates. Chances are that if there is even the slightest trace of a black rim it will, in time, encircle the entire eye. This *could*, however, take as long as four years! If no black eye liner is present on a six- to eight-weeks-old puppy, one cannot say it will never appear. Then again, one cannot say that it will, either!

PINK NOSE

Pink pigmentation on a black nose is considered hopeless by many novice breeders. A butterfly nose usually fills in all black, but it can take as long as a year or even longer to do so. Some puppies that go unsold as old as five or six months because their noses are nearly all pink later develop solid black noses. So don't sell too quickly and pass up what could turn out to be your very own top show dog!

COLOR AND GROOMING

Even grooming can affect the color of your Old English Sheepdog. You must take special care not to remove the undercoat for fear of grooming it out entirely, thus altering the color and appearance of the dog, since the undercoat is usually a different shade from the outer coat, which gives the dog the correct Sheepdog look.

CORRECT SIZE IN THE OLD ENGLISH SHEEPDOG

The trend toward "bigger" and supposedly better Sheepdogs has been going on for at least a decade!

In the show ring there seems to be a definite preference for the larger Sheepdogs, which is probably the reason for the big-dog vogue. One begins to feel like a loser upon entering the ring when one's own dog meets the Standard and yet seems lost among giants ahead of and behind him. We believe the Sheepdog was not intended to be a giant, but rather a dog of sheeplike size that blended in nicely with a flock of sheep.

He can travel faster and better if his size is kept at the Standard requirement. The larger specimens cannot turn as fast, nor as sharp, and we see smaller Sheepdogs used for working in their

An Old English Sheepdog puppy of pet quality. The white patch on the back is undesirable.

natural setting. Even sheepdogs of other breeds are of a medium-size: i.e., Collies, etc.

In breeding for the correct Standard-type Old English Sheepdog, we must remember the dog's intended purpose was not to impress anyone as a mighty elephant-size heap of hair in the show ring, but to qualify as a great herd dog of strength and endurance, with stocky build and a sturdy compactness to his body to allow for effortless movement. These qualities seldom are seen in the larger Old English Sheepdogs.

The preferred weight for Old English females should be about sixty-five to eighty-five pounds, with males weighing in at an average of eight-five to ninety. Many of today's champions are as large as Saint Bernards and weigh well over one hundred pounds!

Equally undesirable is the reverse of the aforementioned "over-sized" Old English. . . . small, spindly-looking dogs. This is just as wrong for the breed as the giant, and certainly not the kind of dogs the shepherds would have bred to help them tend their flocks.

EYES

The Old English Sheepdog should have two dark brown eyes, as implied in the Standard. More and more frequently, however, we see light brown eyes or the objectionable yellow eyes. A wall, or china blue eye is becoming quite common and is typical according to the Standard.

When the time comes to determine eye color, examine your young puppies outdoor in bright daylight. While all puppies are born with blue eyes, the eyes should start to darken to brown at

Two Beau Cheval puppies pose on a table for this photograph to show that the coat is black and white on all newborn puppies. The gray comes in later. . . .

around six weeks of age. Therefore, it will be possible to judge good eye color at this age.

CATARACTS IN THE OLD ENGLISH— A BREED THREAT

Cataracts are becoming more and more a reality in our breed. Since we know them to be an inherited recessive trait, it becomes more than ever a breeding obligation to eliminate this problem. From data gathered from a preliminary study, reported in the January, 1972 issue of the *Journal of the American Animal Hospital Association*, cataracts and retinal detachment indicated that this condition may reflect the beginning of a serious breed problem.

Cataracts, which are an opacity of the lens, are a common ocular condition in many breeds. There are any number of causes, both inheritance and injury, and the only successful treatment is the surgical removal of the cataractous lens. There are eight kinds of cataracts, and a diagnosis should be made before surgery to determine whether the condition is one that could improve the sight.

TAIL DOCKING

For the amusement of all we include the following excerpt from the June issue of the 1941 *National Geographic Magazine*. In an article by Freeman Lloyd entitled, "Working Dogs of the World," he wrote in part:

"The Old English Sheepdog is commonly known as the Bobtail, since his tail is bobbed or cut off close to the rump. This dog carries an enormous coat, and a long hairy tail would gather so much mud as to impede the free movement of a hardworking farm dog. Many are born tailless or with short bobs. For the last fifty years, to my own knowledge, this breed has been producing long-tailed, short-tailed and tailless puppies, often in the same litter."

The accompanying photograph of an oil painting of the breed in this issue of the *Geographic* states in part: "Some are natural-born bobtails, but others are made so by docking the tail at the first joint when the puppy is three or four days old."

A little more than a quarter of a century later, the authors of this book must say that to the best of our knowledge and experience Old English Sheepdogs are born with long tails, just as most other dogs, although there have been stories about tailless puppies from some breeders. And we have had one request from an interested buyer who wanted a Sheepdog with the tail left on, so you see there is some question about it! Her request for a Bobtail with a tail she explained was necessary because she lived on a mountain top and the tail would act as a rudder and keep the dog down . . . whatever she meant by that!

But actually, the Old English Sheepdog does not need a tail. In fact, he is better off without it for many reasons, the main one being for cleanliness! All breeds heavily coated in the area under the tail—and the Old English certainly qualifies in this category—have the problem of having excrement clinging to the fur under the tail if the hair is not cut away. This is a probability even when the tail is bobbed. Imagine what it would be if the tail were left long and shaggy!

Mr. Freeman Lloyd was right about one thing, though. At three or four days of age, unless you have a litter of particularly weak, sickly or premature puppies, the tails should be docked. Tail docking is a job for the veterinarian, since it is a surgical operation. The breeder is always the best advisor on just exactly where to cut, so be prepared to know where the proper spot is. The tail is cropped with a sharp instrument, at the first joint, or as close to the root as possible. Usually, one, possibly two, stitches are required, and the healing process follows. The slight pain passes, and once the puppies are back with their mothers all is forgotten.

Dew claws should be removed and cauterized at this time also. If the veterinarian performs this service in your home or in your kennel, make sure the dam is out of earshot. She will be very upset if she hears the puppies whimper, and you don't want to risk her getting so upset that her milk sours and you might then have to feed all those babies from a bottle yourself!

Bleeding can be profuse, and this can tend to upset the mother as well, so it is best to watch the puppies closely for a half hour or so if the mother isn't missing them too much. Start putting the puppies back with the mother as soon as you notice that the bleeding has stopped.

As mentioned before, work with your veterinarian when the time comes to cut the tails. While a qualified veterinarian is the best judge of health and surgical procedure, he is not necessarily

Beau Cheval's first litter of Old English Sheepdogs. Perri-Winkle, Mrs. Minniver and Muffin. Of the three, two were shown and became champions.

an expert on each breed and its requirements. Some veterinarians are inclined to leave the tails too long—so that the bobtail grows up looking rather like a Cocker Spaniel. If you intend to show your Sheepdog, a tail that is too long will have to be shortened; at the age at which a show ring career would be started, this tail shortening would mean major surgery, not to mention the soreness involved. The breeder, therefore, should be knowledgeable about the correct joint at which to cut and preferably should use a veterinarian which another Old English breeder uses.

Meanwhile, the authors would be interested in hearing about any Bobtails born with bobbed tails!

CHAPTER 7

GROOMING YOUR OLD ENGLISH SHEEPDOG

Regardless of how conscientious, sincere or determined new Sheepdog owners are, a very high percentage will have allowed their dogs to become matted, dirty, and almost beyond the help of brushing by the time the dogs have become a year of age.

This breed is one that requires more grooming than most other breeds. The work involved in keeping an Old English Sheepdog in top show condition is almost endless. But IF you have done a good job, this concentrated effort can be most rewarding later on in the show ring!

The result of a neglected Old English is usually a complete shaving down to the skin, removing the entire coat for the dog's comfort and to the owner's shame!

GROOMING THE OLD ENGLISH SHEEPDOG PUPPY

The easiest way to start with a brand new puppy is to begin on a low table. An old table cut down to coffee table height is appropriate and comfortable for you to sit or kneel next to when breaking in six- to twelve-weeks-old puppies. If the table is at this height the puppy will not fear the height and be restless right from the start. If you begin with the regular grooming table you will have to keep reassuring the puppy if he shows any evidence of fear and will have to guard against its jumping off into space in an attempt to escape the threat of grooming and/or falling.

The puppy should be soothed and loved while being brushed. Great patience is necessary, since it is difficult for young puppies to remain still for any length of time without getting restless and fretful. If you notice the puppy getting bored or tired, try at this point to start the training for grooming with the dog lying on its side. This will be difficult, perhaps, but will save endless time for the months and months of grooming ahead and will not be as tiring for the dog.

The best way to break a puppy in to this is starting by laying it on its back between your legs at the age of three weeks. This is an excellent position for cutting the nails and checking teeth and rubbing stomachs! This original, almost-play position, can lead nicely into rolling the dog over on its side while you begin to brush.

The Old English Sheepdog puppy should be groomed once a day up until the time it is one year old. At that time, however, a more serious type of brushing becomes necessary, but it need be done only about once a week. Since serious matting does not occur until about nine months of age, a daily brushing will keep the coat in good shape and should not require too much time if done daily. This daily care, plus one or two baths during puppyhood, which will help make the dead hair disappear, should keep the puppy in fine shape if it is kept in the house or in clean kennel quarters.

Clean dogs are much easier to take care of and are less likely to tangle. If you intend to take your puppy to dog shows, bathe it one week or less before the show date. The day before does not give the coat time to get back its natural "oil" and to be restored to its natural texture. Feet can be powdered after being wet down and brushed dry for last minute emergencies the day of the show. Just be sure all traces of powder or cornstarch are brushed out thoroughly before entering the show ring. If the judge discovers powder in the coat he'll disqualify your entry.

GROOMING THE ADULT OLD ENGLISH SHEEPDOG

Let us assume you have a slightly matted Old English which is in need of a good grooming. Stand the dog—if you have trained your dog to jump up onto the table it will be a great help and much easier on your back—on the table you use for grooming and make sure the table is steady. The table should be covered with ribbed rubber matting or some other equally non-slide

Stage and movie star Burgess Meredith and his co-star Margalo Gilmore in a scene from the stage production of **The Barretts of Wimpole Street,** with the Old English Sheepdog Snow Bob of Merriedip. Aside from being a stage star, the dog is a show dog as well!

material. If you use a grooming pole, this is the time the head should be slipped through the noose and attached at a comfortable height for the dog. Test for looseness by placing your fingers within the noose at the dog's throat to see that there is space between the noose and the neck.

If you have one groomer for each side of the dog, lucky you! It automatically cuts the time in half and offers conversation at the same time. A radio helps too! Have your grooming utensils handy either in an apron or in the center of the table.

Completely brush the dog out, patiently removing all the mats. Each mat must be taken into the fingers and gently separated, slowly and carefully tearing it into smaller tangles, brushing gently in between tearings. As the mat comes nearer to the ends of the hair, a comb may be used to gently work it to the end of the hair and out. This process can be long and even painful to the dog if the matting is very bad, but if the dog complains too much YOU must be doing something wrong. Either you are too rough or not holding the hair near the skin as you tug away at the tangles. Gently does it! For huge mats, softening with a spray of water or creme hair rinse specially prepared for dogs will help.

Mat splitters, a wide toothed comb, and a pin brush will do the trick and not be painful if properly used. Hopefully, the breeder of your dog will instruct you in this procedure if there is any doubt in your mind, or if you seem to be pulling out too much coat. The pin brush can pierce the skin if you are too rough, so be especially careful of it, particularly around the eyes and "private" areas.

Spraying the dog with water and brushing dry with either powder or cornstarch will help keep your dog clean. Also, there are dry shampoos available at pet shops for those in-between time baths. But if your Bobtail likes to romp outdoors there will be times when a full bath is absolutely necessary!

BATHING THE OLD ENGLISH SHEEPDOG

The dog should be brushed out *before* a bath. Then, before removing the dog from the table and placing it in the tub, apply eye ointment to the eyes to prevent the soap from burning them.

Hopefully your tub will be one of the two-section type which will prevent the dog from sitting or lying down in the tub. Place two feet in each side of either a half full or empty tub. Then thoroughly wet down the dog with hose and running warm water. Soak thoroughly to the skin in all areas, saving the head for last. Part the hair on the head and pour the water back from the face to keep the water out of the eyes as much as possible. If you don't have the short length of hose with a strong spray, a bowl will do.

Once the dog is drenched you will be ready to apply the shampoo. A commercially prepared shampoo especially for dogs is best, since it will undoubtedly contain the proper protein and conditioners. Suds are worked up to a lather to the point that the hair should stand up in peaks. Pay particular attention to soaping the whiskers on the chin, since this and the area under the tail are always the dirtiest! (Except maybe the feet!) Take care not to tangle the coat any more than is necessary during the sudsing by gently squeezing the lather through the hair rather than rubbing or moving in a circular motion.

When you are sure that the dog is clean—including those elbows and hocks—it is time to start your rinsings. Again, using your hose, thoroughly rinse the dog not once, but twice—and then a third time! We cannot emphasize too strongly what damage can be done by leaving soap in the coat. Once you are convinced that the rinsing is over and you have cleaned the face thoroughly with a wet rag to catch the water drippings from the excess hair, you are ready to get the turkish towels into action for the squeeze-drying process.

While the dog is still in the tub, dripping and with a shake or two, throw a towel over him and start squeezing the coat very gently. Do not rub! Squeeze all over and do the feet last, just before lifting the dog over onto the grooming table once again. If you feel the dog needs to "go," this is the time to take care of it, before the serious grooming and drying begins. He'll be restless if he has to go and you don't let him, but at the same time don't let him pick up a lot of dirt outside making up his mind.

THE DRYING PROCESS

A quick, gentle over-all brushing while you use the hand dryer or a professional dog dryer is a good beginning. Have your scissors ready for the shaping which must be done. After the legs and feet have been carefully brushed, comb out the hair on each foot. All the hair between the toes and pads should be carefully cut out with a rounded scissors. Shape and brush the feet like large ROUND powder puffs. Repeat this process several times if necessary until they are right.

Many Sheepdog owners do not trim or scissor the rump, and we see little of this in other countries. However, we feel it can add greatly to the appeal of the dog. If you are inexperienced, and until you are quite sure you know how to do it yourself, it would be advisable to have another Sheepdog owner or a groomer do it for you. Scissoring the rump has been known to make the difference between winning or losing at a show. It can add, or detract, so much from the conformation of the Sheepdog!

If you do it yourself, use the nubbin of the tail as your guide. Trim and round out the shape of the rump slowly, carefully and a little at a time, until no hair is longer than the end of the tail. Keep brushing the hair on the back and rump toward the tail and continue cutting. Having the hair around the rectum scissored, your dog will have a cleaner rear and a shaplier rump.

Next, cut and shape the hair on the rear hocks so they are not straggly looking. Cut and round the paws also. The look of the legs and feet should appear as ONE with no break at the pastern or wrist joint. The entire leg should like look one extremely heavy bone.

For after-bath grooming, you still should be using the steel pin with rubber base brush. A comb with teeth set wide apart as well as one with teeth close together will also be needed. You will be using your combs on the feet, ears, face, beard, elbows, and "touchy" spots, such as the vulva on the bitch and the scrotum on the dog.

The body hair is brushed as follows: the back is brushed forward. The head is brushed forward and down. The neck and shoulders are brushed forward. The legs are brushed up. The chest is brushed forward and down. The rump is brushed in a sunburst manner or out from the rectum and tail area forward toward the dog's head.

The head of the dog needs particular attention. All matter should be removed from the eyes, and in this breed, as in others where there is profuse hair in the area of the eyes, a hard crust of dark matter is usually gathered in the corner of the adult dogs' eyes.

Make sure all mats are removed from behind the ears, on the cheeks, muzzle and chin area, and that all hair around the mouth is clean and white. Whitening can be achieved by adding cornstarch while damp and brushing dry. Make sure the nose is washed clean and, if necessary, add the "wet look" by applying vaseline with your fingers.

The bangs or "fall" of hair over the eyes may be tied with a rubber band until show time and then brushed out, but make sure the rubber band does not pull the hair or the dog will not tolerate it and you will lose a lot of hair if he scratches it out. Some apply this process to the beard and ears as well, but most

Sheepdogs will not tolerate this for long.

The head should look like a chrysanthemum, and this can be effected by backbrushing the hair on the cheeks, ears, and top of the head, and then brushing forward as directed above.

THE EARS

All long hairs should be pulled out from inside the ear canal, or cut gently with little scissors. The wax and dirt should be cleaned out with cotton dipped in alcohol, or with cotton swabs.

CLIPPING OR SHAVING THE OLD ENGLISH SHEEPDOG

Shudder to think of it, but if your Sheepdog has gotten beyond repair in the grooming department, the easiest and fastest course of action to give the dog comfort is clipping or shaving. The worse the condition of the dog, the closer to the skin you must clip. And you will want to clip in an even pattern so that the coat, when it does come back in, will not be ragged and full of holes.

Pet shops carry clippers for this clipping and shaving process. Since you hope this will never happen again, we suggest you might even borrow the clippers or have it done in a grooming parlor by a professional. You should watch it being done so that should it become absolutely necessary to do it again, you will be somewhat knowledgeable about the process and how to go about it.

It is easier than you might think to nick, cut or even burn a dog with clippers. So it is wise, if you buy your clippers, to ask for instructions at the place of purchase, or to ask assistance and instruction from an Old English Sheepdog owner who has done this before.

In some homes where Bobtails are to be kept only as pets, owners have the dog clipped periodically and keep the coat at about one to four inches in length over the entire body. The dog keeps nicely, is comfortable, looks nice and doesn't get into the advanced state of bad tangles and matting. This is called the "Fun Clip" by many and still provides the typical shaggy Old English Sheepdog appearance while the dog can swim, run through the

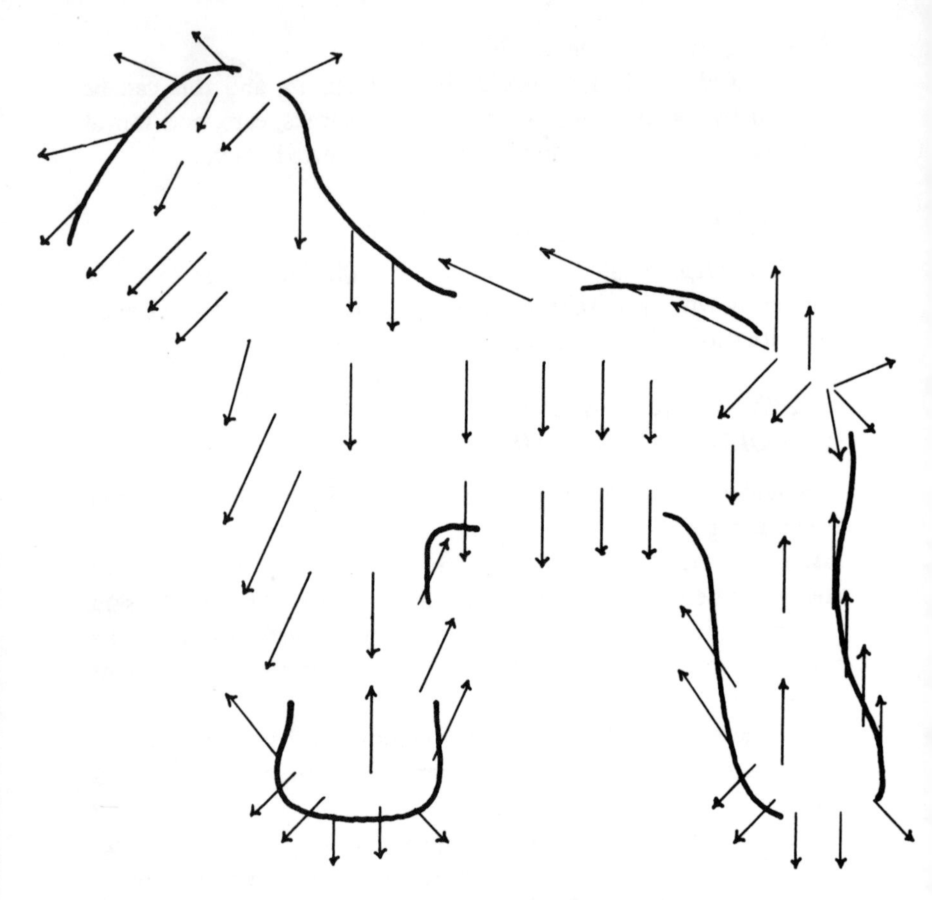

ARROWS INDICATE IN WHICH DIRECTION THE HAIR SHOULD BE BRUSHED WHEN GROOMING THE OLD ENGLISH SHEEPDOG

fields and roughhouse with friends and family without severely damaging his coat.

For family pets the Fun Clip is hard to beat, since it takes the daily grooming routine into the realm of twice a week grooming without giving every member of the family guilt feelings about neglect of the natural long coat. All you need do is scissor twice a year or so . . . and you and all your friends will still recognize the dog as an Old English Sheepdog!

CHAPTER 8

GENETICS

No one can guarantee nature! But, with facts and theories at your command you can at least, on paper, plan a litter of puppies that should fulfill your fondest expectations. Since the ultimate purpose of breeding is to try to improve the breed, this planning, no matter how uncertain, should be earnestly attempted.

There are a few terms you should be familiar with to help you understand the breeding procedure and the structure of genetics. The first thing that comes to mind is the Mendelian Law—or The Laws of Mendelian Inheritance. Who was Mendel? Gregor Mendel was an Austrian clergyman and botanist born in Brunn, Moravia. He developed his basic theories on heredity while working with peas. Not realizing the full import of his work, he published a paper on his experiments in a scientific journal in the year 1866. That paper went unnoticed for many years, but the laws and theories put forth in it have been tried and proven. Today they are accepted by scientists as well as dog breeders.

To help understand the Mendelian law as it applies to breeding dogs, we must acquaint ourselves with certain scientific terms and procedures. First of all, dogs possess glands of reproduction which are called gonads. The gonads of the male are in the testicles which produce sperm, or spermatozoa. The gonads of the female are the ovaries and produce eggs. The bitch is born with these eggs and, when she is old enough to reproduce, she comes into heat. The eggs descend from the ovaries via the Fallopian tubes to the two horns of the uterus. There they either pass on out during the heat cycle or are fertilized by the male sperm in the semen deposited during a mating.

In dog mating, there is what we refer to as a tie, which is a time period during which the male pumps about 600 million spermatozoa into the female to fertilize the ripened eggs. When the sperm and the ripe eggs meet, zygotes are created and the little one-celled

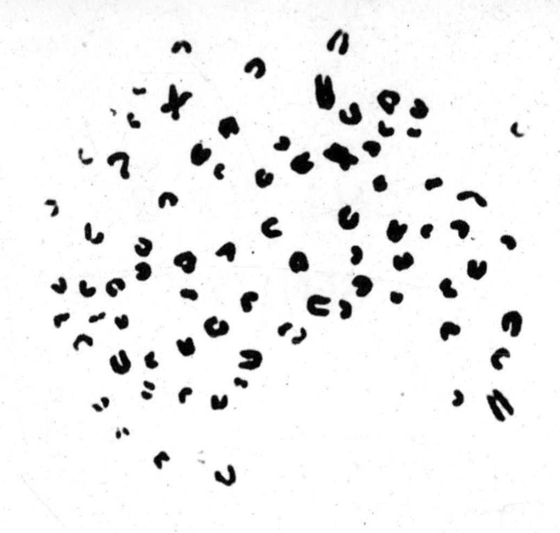

The dog has 78 chromosomes while man has 46 and the cat has 38. The two members of each pair of chromosomes look alike except for the sex chromosomes. A female has two large X chromosomes (see lower right in the illustration). The male has one X chromosome and a small Y chromosome which is the determinant for maleness. The preparation pictured above was made from a white blood cell of a female Keeshond. The chromosomes have been paired according to size.

Droverdale Fogbound Pirate, owned by Phil and Arlene Gavin. Pirate had 14 points toward his championship at the time this photograph was taken.

future puppies descend from the Fallopian tubes into the uterus where they attach themselves to the walls of the uterus and begin to develop. With all inherited characteristics determined as the zygote was formed, the dam now must only assume her role as incubator for her babies, which are now organisms in their own right. The bitch has been bred and is now in whelp!

Let us take a closer look at what is happening during the breeding phenomenon. We know that while the male deposits as many as 600 million sperm into the female, the number of ripe eggs she releases will determine the number of puppies in the litter. Therefore, those breeders who advertise their stud as "producer of large litters" do not know the facts. The bitch determines the size of the litter; the male the sex of the puppies. It takes only one sperm of the 600 million to produce a puppy.

Each dog and bitch possesses 39 pairs of chromosomes in each reproductive germ cell. The chromosomes carry the genes, like peas in a pod, and there are approximately 150,000 genes in each chromosome. These chromosomes split apart and unite with half the chromosomes from the other parent and the puppy's looks and temperament are created.

To understand the procedure more thoroughly, we must understand that there are two kinds of genes—dominant and recessive. A dominant gene is one of a pair whose influence is expressed to the exclusion of the effects of the other. A recessive gene is one of a pair whose influence is subdued by the effects of the other. Most of the important qualities we wish to perpetuate in our breeding programs are carried on by the dominant genes. It is the successful breeder who becomes expert at eliminating recessive or undesirable genes and building up the dominant or desirable genes. This principle holds true in every phase of breeding—inside and outside the dog!

There are many excellent books available which will take you deeper into the fascinating subject of canine genetics. You can learn about your chances of getting so many black, so many white, and so many black and white puppies, etc. Avail yourself of this information before your next—or hopefully, first—breeding. We have merely touched upon genetics here to point out the importance of planned parenthood. Any librarian can help you find further information, or books may be purchased offering the very latest findings in canine genetics. It is a fascinating and rewarding program toward creating better dogs.

CHAPTER 9

BREEDING YOUR OLD ENGLISH SHEEPDOG

Let us assume the time has come for your dog to be bred, and you have decided you are in a position to enjoy producing a litter of puppies that you hope will make a contribution to the breed. The bitch you purchased is sound, her temperament is excellent and she is a most worthy representative of the breed.

You have taken a calendar and counted off the ten days since the first day of red staining and have determined the tenth to 14th day which will more than likely be the best days for the actual mating. You have additionally counted off 59–63 days before the puppies will be born to make sure everything necessary for their arrival will be in good order by that time.

From the moment the idea of having a litter occurred to you, your thoughts should have been given to the correct selection of a proper stud. Here again the novice would do well to seek advice on analyzing pedigrees and tracing bloodlines for your best breedings. As soon as the bitch is in season and you see color (or staining) and a swelling of the vulva, it is time to notify the owner of the stud you selected and make appointments for the breedings. There are several pertinent questions you will want to ask the stud owner after having decided upon the pedigree.

THE HEALTH OF THE BREEDING STOCK

Some of your first questions should be: Has this adult male ever sired a litter? Has his sperm count been checked? Has he been X-rayed for Hip Dysplasia and found to be clear? Does he have two normal-sized testicles? Do not be impressed with the owner's romantic tales of his "Romeo" behavior. You can hear just as many stories about the amorous male that thinks he's a stud, but has never yet made a successful tie. Ask if he needs human assistance to complete a breeding and what his score is on the number of breedings that have produced a litter. Is he a lazy or aggressive stud; in other words, does he give up easily if the bitch does not cooperate?

When considering your bitch for this mating, you must take into consideration a few important points that lead to a successful breeding. Has she had normal heat cycles? Four months may be normal for some, but six or nine months is normal for most. Has she ever been bred before and what were the results? Did she have normal puppies? Too many runts—mis-marks, brown noses, etc.? Has she ever had a vaginal infection? Did she have a normal delivery and did the pregnancy go its full term? Did she have to have one or more Caesarean sections? Was she a good mother, and did she have a lot of milk, or none at all? Did she allow assistance during delivery? Did the puppies all survive or did you lose several from the litter shortly after birth?

Don't buy a bitch that has problem heats and never a litter. And don't be afraid to buy a healthy maiden bitch, since chances are, if she is healthy and from good stock, she will be a healthy producer for you. Don't buy a monorchid male, or one with a low sperm count. Any veterinarian can give you a count and you will do well to require one, especially if it is to be the stud dog for a kennel. Older dogs that have been good producers and are for sale are usually not too hard to find at good established kennels. If they are not too old and have sired show quality puppies, they can give you some excellent litters from which to establish your breeding stock from solid bloodlines.

THE WEDDING DATE

Now that you have decided upon the proper male and female combination to produce what you hope will be—according to the pedigrees—a fine litter of puppies, it is time to set the date. You have selected the two days (with one day lapse in between) that you feel are best for the breeding, and you call the owner of the stud. The bitch always goes to the stud, unless, of course, there are extenuating circumstances and the stud then goes to the female. You set the date and the time and arrive with the dog and the *money*.

Standard procedure is payment of a stud fee at the time of the first breeding, if there is a tie. For the stud fee, you are entitled to two breedings with ties. Contracts may be written up with specific conditions on breeding terms, of course, but this is general pro-

The Old English Sheepdog Club Specialty Show in June, 1971 saw judge Mrs. Mona Berkowitz place Ch. Gwenelog Blue Valley as Best of Breed. Blue Valley was handled by Carol Magyar for owner Norma J. Rockwall. The event was held in Greenwich, Connecticut. Photo by Charles Mintzer.

cedure. Often a breeder will take the pick of a litter to protect and maintain his bloodlines. This can be especially desirable if he needs an outcross for his breeding program. He may also wish to maintain his bloodline if you have originally purchased the bitch from him and the breeding will continue his line-breeding program. This should all be worked out ahead of time and written and signed before the two dogs are bred together. Remember that the payment of the stud fee is for the services of the stud—not for a guarantee of a litter of puppies. This is why it is so important to make sure you are using a proven stud. Bear in mind, also, that the American Kennel Club will not register a litter of puppies sired by a male that is under eight months of age. In the case of the older dog, they will not register a litter sired by a dog over 12 years of age, without a witness to the breeding in the form of a veterinarian or other responsible person.

Many studs over 12 years of age are still fertile and capable of producing puppies, but if you do not witness the breeding there is always the danger of a "substitute" stud being used to produce a litter. This brings up the subject of sending your bitch away to be bred, if you cannot accompany her.

The disadvantages of sending a bitch away to be bred are numerous. First of all, she will not be herself in a strange place and may be difficult to handle. Transportation—if she goes by air—while reasonably safe, is still a traumatic experience and there is the danger of her being put off at the wrong airport, not being fed or watered properly, etc. Some bitches get so upset that they go out of season and the trip, which may prove expensive, especially on top of a substantial stud fee, will have been for nothing.

If at all possible, accompany your bitch so that the experience is as comfortable for her as it can be. In other words, make sure before setting this kind of schedule for a breeding that there is no stud in the area that might be as good for her as the one that is far away. We do not wish to have you sacrifice the proper breeding for convenience, since bloodlines are so important, but we do put the safety of the bitch above all else. There is always a risk in traveling, since dogs are considered cargo on a plane.

HOW MUCH DOES THE STUD FEE COST?

The stud fee will vary considerably—the better the bloodlines, the more winning the dog does at shows, the higher the fee. A top winning dog could run up to $500. Here again, there may be exceptions. Some breeders will take part cash and then, say, third or fourth pick of the litter. The fee can be arranged by a private contract, rather than the traditional procedure we have described.

ARTIFICIAL INSEMINATION

Breeding by means of artificial insemination is usually unsuccessful, unless under a veterinarian's supervision, and can lead to an infection for the bitch and discomfort for the dog. The American Kennel Club requires a veterinarian's certificate to register puppies from such a breeding. Although the practice has been used for over

Robert and Sadie Hawkins' gorgeous Strategic Air Commando pictured winning over 17 Bobtails at the Detroit show in March, 1963 under judge Maurice Baker. Shown handling for the Hawkinses, who reside in Highland, Michigan, is Barbara Humphrey.

This rare candid shot of an Old English Sheepdog with a Veronica Lake hairdo was captured by photographer "Hanks" and never fails to elicit a smile from Bobtail lovers.

Another Ragbear Bobtail beauty winning at the shows. This time it is Ch. Ragbears Bobmar Hillary Mist capturing a top prize under Judge Nelson Groh. A Joan Ludwig photograph.

two decades, it now offers new promise since research has been conducted to make it a more feasible procedure for the future.

Great dogs may eventually look forward to reproducing themselves years after they have left this earth. There now exists a frozen semen concept that has been tested and works. The study, headed by Dr. Stephen W. J. Seager, M.V.B., and instructor at the University of Oregon Medical School, has the financial support of the American Kennel Club, indicating that organization's interest in the work. The study is being monitored by the Morris Animal Foundation, Denver, Colo.

Dr. Seager announced in 1970 he had been able to preserve dog semen and to produce litters with the stored semen. The possibilities of selective, world-wide breedings by this method are exciting. Imagine simply mailing a vial of semen to the bitch! The perfection of line-breeding by storing semen without the threat of death interrupting the breeding program is exciting also.

As it stands today, the technique for artificial insemination requires the depositing of semen (taken directly from the dog) into the bitch's vagina, past the cervix and into the uterus by syringe. The correct temperature of the semen is vital, and there is no guarantee of success.

The storage method, if adopted, will present a new era in the field of purebred dogs.

THE GESTATION PERIOD

Once the breeding has taken place successfully, the seemingly endless waiting period of 63 days begins. For the first ten days after the breeding, you do absolutely nothing for the bitch—just spin dreams about the delights you will share with the family when the puppies arrive.

Around the tenth day it is time to begin supplementing the diet of the bitch with vitamins and calcium. We strongly recommend that you take her to your veterinarian for a list of the proper supplements and the correct amounts for your particular bitch. Guesses, which may lead to excesses or insufficiencies, can ruin a litter. For the price of a visit to your veterinarian, you will be confident that you are feeding properly.

The bitch should be free of worms, of course, and if there is any doubt in your mind, she should be wormed now, before the third week of pregnancy. Your veterinarian will advise you on the necessity of this as well.

PROBING FOR PUPPIES

Far too many breeders are overanxious about whether the breeding "took" and are inclined to feel for puppies or persuade a

Photographed in 1942, these adorable shaggy Merriedip puppies were owned by Mrs. H. M. Lewis of Massachusetts and New York.

veterinarian to radiograph or X-ray their bitches to confirm it. Unless there is reason to doubt the normalcy of a pregnancy, this is risky. Certainly 63 days are not too long to wait, and why risk endangering the litter by probing with your inexperienced hands? Few bitches give no evidence of being in whelp, and there is no need to prove it for yourself by trying to count puppies.

ALERTING YOUR VETERINARIAN

At least a week before the puppies are due, you should telephone your veterinarian and notify him that you expect the litter and give him the date. This way he can make sure that there will be someone available to help, should there be any problems during the whelping. Most veterinarians today have answering services and alternate veterinarians on call when they are not available themselves. Some vets suggest that you call them when the bitch starts labor so that they may further plan their time, should they be needed. Discuss this matter with him when you first take the bitch to him for her diet instructions, etc., and establish the method which will best fit in with his schedule.

DO YOU NEED A VETERINARIAN IN ATTENDANCE?

Even if this is your first litter, we would advise that you go through the experience of whelping without panicking and calling desperately for the veterinarian. Most animal births are accomplished without complications, and you should call for assistance only if you run into trouble.

When having her puppies your bitch will appreciate as little interference and as few strangers around as possible. A quiet place, with her nest, a single familiar face and her own instincts are all that is necessary for nature to take its course. An audience of curious children squealing and questioning, other family pets nosing around, or strange adults should be avoided. Many a bitch who has been distracted in this way has been known to devour her young. This can be the horrible result of intrusion of the bitch's privacy. There are other ways of teaching children the miracle of birth, and there will be plenty of time later for the whole family to enjoy the puppies. Let them be born under proper and considerate circumstances.

LABOR

Some litters—many first litters—do not run the full term of 63 days. So, at least a week before the puppies are actually due, and at the time you alert your veterinarian as to their arrival, start observing the bitch for signs of the commencement of labor. This will manifest itself in the form of ripples running down the sides of her body, which will come as a revelation to her as well. It is most noticeable when she is lying on her side—and she will be sleeping a great deal as the arrival date comes closer. If she is sitting or walking about, she will perhaps sit down quickly or squat peculiarly. When you notice this for the first time, your vigil has begun. As the ripples become more frequent, birth time is drawing near and you will be wise not to leave her. Usually within 24 hours before whelping, she will stop eating, and as much as a week before, she will begin digging a nest. The bitch should be given something resembling a whelping box with layers of newspaper (black and white only) to make her nest. She will dig more and more as birth approaches and this is the time to begin making your promise to stop interfering unless your help is specifically required. Some bitches whimper, others are silent, but whimpering does not necessarily indicate trouble.

THE ARRIVAL OF THE PUPPIES

The sudden gush of green fluid from the bitch indicates that the water or fluid surrounding the puppies has "broken" and they are about to start down the canal and come into the world.When the water breaks, birth of the first puppy is imminent. The first puppies are usually born within minutes to a half hour of each other, but a couple of hours between the later ones is not uncommon. If you notice the bitch straining constantly without producing a puppy, or if a puppy remains partially in and partially out for too long, it is cause for concern. Breech births (puppies born feet instead of head first) can often cause delay or hold things up, and this is often a problem which requires veterinary assistance.

FEEDING THE BITCH BETWEEN BIRTHS

Usually the bitch will not be interested in food for about 24 hours before the arrival of the puppies, and perhaps as long as two or three days after their arrival. The placenta which she cleans up after each puppy is high in food value and will be more than ample to sustain her. This is nature's way of allowing the mother to feed herself and her babies without having to leave the nest and hunt for food during the first crucial days. The mother always cleans up all traces of birth in the wilds so as not to attract other animals to her newborn babies.

However, there are those of us who believe in making food available, should the mother feel the need to restore her strength during or after delivery—especially if she whelps a large litter. Raw chopmeat, beef bouillon, and milk are all acceptable and may be placed near the whelping box during the first two or three days. After that, the mother will begin to put the babies on a sort of schedule. She will leave the whelping box at frequent intervals, take longer exercise periods, and begin to take interest in other things. This is where the fun begins for you. Now the babies are no longer soggy

Send us a photo* of your dog...and we'll return a color masterpiece you'll treasure for life.

Your favorite photo recreated on a special 8" x 10" canvas-textured finish.

Purina Dog Meal, the super-energy meal specially formulated for show dogs, brood bitches and hunters.

NOW, for just $2.75 and either one 50-lb. or two 25-lb. Purina Dog Meal weight circles, you can get this beautiful color enlargement of your dog or dogs. And there's no limit . . . you can order as many as you want. Colors and details are sharp and clear . . . but softly textured . . . like an oil painting. Just send us your favorite negative or slide, and we'll return an 8" x 10" portrait ideal for framing or hanging in home or office.

Use this order form, or pick up one where Purina Dog Meal is sold.

Gentlemen: Enclosed are_______negatives or slides, plus either two 25-lb. Purina Dog Meal weight circles *or* one 50-lb. weight circle for each photo enlargement I have ordered. Also enclosed is $2.75** for each photo enlargement I have ordered. Please send me_______enlargements of each print I have enclosed and paid for.

***IMPORTANT:** Send color negatives or slides. *Snapshots not sufficient.* (For black and white enlargements send black and white negative.) Originals will be returned.

***Please send check or money order. No cash or stamps, please. Protect your original with proper wrapping.*

Name____________________Address____________________

City/State/Zip____

SEND ORDER TO: Purina Dog Portrait Offer, Box 3395
New York, New York 10007

Ralston Purina Company handles negatives without warranty or liability.
Allow three weeks for delivery. Offer expires June 30, 1971.

This adorable photograph of a mother Old English Sheepdog and her two puppies was part of a very successful promotion featured by the Ralston-Purina Company to promote one of the company's dog foods. It serves as another example of how "Bobtail conscious" the dog fancy has become during the 1970's.

A look of sheer joy is evident on Leigh Ann Swanson's face as she discovers her new Old English Sheepdog puppy under the Christmas tree. This charming photograph was distributed by the Ken-L Ration company along with instructions on how to care for Christmas puppies.

little pinkish blobs. They begin to crawl around and squeal and hum and grow before your very eyes!

It is at this time, if all has gone normally, that the family can be introduced gradually and great praise and affection given to the mother.

BREECH BIRTHS

Puppies normally are delivered head first. However, some are presented feet first and this is referred to as a "breech birth." Assistance is often necessary to get the puppy out of the canal, and great care must be taken not to injure the puppy or the dam.

Aid can be given by grasping the puppy with a piece of turkish toweling and pulling gently during the dam's contractions. Be

A lovely litter of five-weeks-old Old English Sheepdog puppies bred by Gail Fletcher of Tucson, Arizona. This was Ch. Jendowers Queen Victoria's first litter, and the sire was Ch. Rivermist Dan Tatters.

careful not to squeeze the puppy too hard; merely try to ease it out by moving it gently back and forth. Because even this much delay in delivery may mean the puppy is drowning, do not wait for the bitch to remove the sac. Do it yourself by tearing the sac open to expose the face and head. Then cut the cord anywhere from one-half to three-quarters of an inch away from the navel. If the cord bleeds excessively, pinch the end of it with your fingers and count five. Repeat if necessary. Then pry open the mouth with your finger and hold the puppy upsidedown for a moment to drain any fluids from the lungs. Next, rub the puppy briskly with turkish or paper toweling. You should get wriggling and whimpering by this time.

If the litter is large, this assistance will help conserve the strength of the bitch and will probably be welcomed by her. However, it is best to allow her to take care of at least the first few herself to preserve the natural instinct, and to provide the nutritive values obtained by her consumption of the afterbirths.

DRY BIRTHS

Occasionally, the sac will break before the delivery of a puppy and will be expelled while the puppy remains inside, thereby depriving the dam of the necessary lubrication to expel the puppy normally. Inserting vaseline or mineral oil via your finger will help the puppy pass down the birth canal. This is why it is essential that you be present during the whelping so that you can count puppies and afterbirths and determine when and if assistance is needed.

THE TWENTY-FOUR-HOUR CHECKUP

It is smart to have a veterinarian check the mother and her puppies within 24 hours after the last puppy is born. The veterinarian can check for a cleft palate or umbilical hernia and may wish to give the dam—particularly if she is a show dog—an injection of Pituitin to make sure of the expulsion of all afterbirths and to tighten up the uterus. This can prevent a sagging belly after the puppies are weaned and the bitch is being readied for the show ring.

FALSE PREGNANCY

The disappointment of a false pregnancy is almost as bad for the owner as it is for the bitch. She goes through the entire 63 days with all the symptoms—swollen stomach, increased appetite, swollen nipples—even makes a nest when the time comes. You may even take an oath that you noticed the ripples on her body from the labor pains. Then, just as suddenly as you made up your mind that she was definitely going to have puppies, you will know that she definitely is not! She may walk around carrying a toy as if it were a puppy for a few days, but she will soon be back to normal and acting just as if nothing happened—and nothing did!

CAESAREAN SECTION

Should the whelping reach the point where there is a complication, such as the bitch not being capable of whelping the puppies herself, the "moment of truth" is upon you and a Caesarean section may be necessary. The bitch may be too small or too immature to expel the puppies herself; or her cervix may fail to dilate enough to

A boy and his dog, photographed by Percy T. Jones in 1950.

allow the young to come down the birth canal; or there may be torsion of the uterus, a dead or monster puppy, a sideways puppy blocking the canal, or perhaps toxemia. A Caesarean section will be the only solution. No matter what the cause, get the bitch to the veterinarian immediately to insure your chances of saving the mother and/or the puppies.

The Caesarean section operation (the name derived from the legend that Julius Caesar was delivered into the world by this method) involves the removal of the unborn young from the uterus of the dam by surgical incision into the walls through the abdomen. The operation is performed when it has been determined that for some reason the puppies cannot be delivered normally. While modern surgical methods have made the operation itself reasonably safe, with the dam being perfectly capable of nursing the puppies shortly after the completion of the surgery, the chief danger lies in the ability to spark life into the puppies immediately upon their removal from the womb. If the mother dies, the time element is even more important in saving the young, since the oxygen supply

A litter of Merriedip puppies with proud dam and sire.

ceases upon the death of the dam, and the difference between life and death is measured in seconds.

After surgery when the bitch is home in her whelping box with the babies, she will probably nurse the young without distress. You must be sure that the sutures are kept clean and that no redness or swelling or ooze appears in the wound. Healing will take place naturally and no salves or ointments should be applied unless prescribed by the veterinarian, for fear the puppies will get it into their systems. Check the bitch for fever if there is any doubt, restlessness, (other than the natural concern for her young) or a lack of appetite, but do not anticipate trouble.

EPISIOTOMY

Even though the large breeds of dogs, such as the Old English, are generally easy whelpers, any number of reasons might occur to cause the bitch to have a difficult birth. Before automatically resorting to Caesarean section, many veterinarians are now trying the technique known as episiotomy.

Used rather frequently in human deliveries, episiotomy (pronounced A-PEASE-E-OTT-O-ME) is the cutting of the membrane between the rear opening of the vagina back almost to the opening of the anus. After delivery it is stitched together, and barring complications, heals easily, presenting no problem in future births.

ORPHAN PUPPIES

Should you experience the misfortune of having a litter of orphaned puppies, either because the dam has died, or is for some reason unwilling or unable to take care of the puppies herself, there is still a good possibility of saving them. With today's substitutes for mother's milk, and with a lot of perseverance on your part, it can be done.

The first step is to take the puppies far enough away from the mother so that their odor and crying does not make her restless or remind her that she is not doing the job herself. The next step is to see that they are kept warm and dry and out of drafts. This can be accomplished by placing them in a deep box on a heating pad in a quiet, secluded spot in the house where there is no bright light to injure their sensitive eyes when they begin to open at anywhere from one to two weeks of age.

Caution! The most important point regarding the heating pad is that you must be absolutely sure it is not too hot. There have been enough reports of "cooked" puppies to turn us into vegetarians! Put the heating pad on its very lowest temperature, cover it with several thicknesses of newspaper and a small baby blanket on top of that. Test it by holding your wrist and inner arm on it steadily for a few minutes to see if the heat is too intense. If it is, more newspaper must be added. There should be barely more than a discernible warmth—not heat. Also make sure that at least a third of the bottom of the box is not covered with the heating pad so that if the heat builds up, the puppy's natural instinct might help them escape to a section of the box which is not heated—just as they would crawl away from the dam if they were too warm or snuggle up to her if they felt the need for warmth. Too much heat also tends to dehydrate the puppies. Make sure, also, the heating pad is well secured so that the puppies do not suffocate under it while moving around in the box.

Now that you have the puppies bedded down properly in a substitute environment comparable to one they would share with their natural mother, you provide the survival diet! Your substitute formula must be precisely prepared, always served heated to body

Linus, the fashion plate! The Leonard Bergsteins' fashion-conscious Old English Sheepdog models a Givenchy scarf and sun glasses at a showing of Bergdoff Goodman clothes in a fashion show at the Pierre Hotel in New York City. Linus created a sensation as he promenaded down the runway. This annual fashion show is for the benefit of New York Animal Medical Center, and each dog is attired in an outfit matching the one his human companion model is wearing. Not only does Linus do his part for this marvelous charity event each year, but further distinguishes himself in the show ring; he is a champion, of course! Photo courtesy of the *New York Post*, whose Fashion Editor, Eugenia Sheppard, reports on the event to her readers each year.

temperature and refrigerated when not being fed. Esbilac, a vacuum-packed powder, with complete feeding instructions on the can, is excellent and about as close to mother's milk as you can get. If you can't get Esbilac, or until you do get Esbilac, there are two alternative formulas that you might use.

Mix one part boiled water with five parts of evaporated milk and add one teaspoonful of di-calcium phosphate per quart of formula. Di-calcium phosphate can be secured at any drug store. If they have it in tablet form only, you can powder the tablets with the back part of a tablespoon. The other formula for newborn puppies is a combination of eight ounces of homogenized milk mixed well with two egg yolks.

You will need baby bottles with the three-hole nipples. Sometimes doll bottles can be used for the newborn puppies, which should be fed at six-hour intervals. If they are consuming sufficient amounts, their stomachs should look full, or slightly enlarged, though never distended. Amount of formula to be fed is proportionate to size and age, and growth and weight of puppy, and is indicated on the can of Esbilac or on the advice of your veterinarian. Many breeders like to keep a baby scale nearby to check the weight of the puppies to be sure they are thriving on the formula.

At two to three weeks you can start adding Pablum or some other high protein baby cereal to the formula. Also, baby beef can be licked from your finger at this age, or added to the formula. At four weeks the surviving puppies should be taken off the diet of Esbilac and put on a more substantial diet, such as wet puppy meal or cereals with chopped beef. However, Esbilac powder can still be mixed in with the food for additional nutrition.

HOW TO FEED THE NEWBORN PUPPIES

When the puppy is a newborn, remember that it is vitally important to keep the feeding procedure as close to the natural mother's routine as possible. The newborn puppy should be held in your hand in an almost upright position with the bottle at an angle to allow the entire nipple area to be full of the formula. Do not hold the bottle upright so the puppy's head has to reach straight up toward the ceiling. Do not let the puppy nurse too quickly or take in too much air and possibly get colic. Once in a while, take the bottle away and let him rest for a moment and swallow several

Fun in the fields! Two brothers enjoy the farm of their owner, Steven Clofine, in Bernville, Pennsylvania.

times. Before feeding, always test the nipple to see that the fluid does not come out too quickly, or by the same token, too slowly so that the puppy gets tired of feeding before he has had enough to eat.

When the puppy is a little older, you can place him on his stomach on a towel to eat, and even allow him to hold on to the bottle or to "come and get it" on his own. Most puppies enjoy eating and this will be a good indication of how strong an appetite he has and his ability to consume the contents of the bottle.

It will be necessary to "burp" the puppy. Place a towel on your shoulder and hold the puppy on your shoulder as if it were a human baby, patting and rubbing it gently. This will also encourage the puppy to defecate. At this time, you should observe for diarrhea or other intestinal disorders. The puppy should eliminate after each feeding with occasional eliminations between times as well. If the puppies do not eliminate on their own after each meal, massage their stomachs and under their tails until they do.

You must be sure to keep the puppies clean. If there is diarrhea the puppy should be washed and dried off. Under no circumstances should fecal matter be allowed to collect on their skin or fur.

All this—plus your determination and perseverance—might save an entire litter of puppies that would otherwise have died without their real mother.

Julie and Ed Broctsch's Droverdale Rogue N' Saint. Rogue went Best of Breed over Specials at just eight months of age. Bred by the Droverdale Old English Sheepdog Kennels in Oxon Hill, Maryland.

WEANING THE PUPPIES

There are many diets today for young puppies, including all sorts of products on the market for feeding the newborn, for supplementing feeding the young and for adding this or that to diets, depending on what is lacking in the way of complete diet.

When weaning puppies, it is necessary to put them on four meals a day, even while you are tapering off with the mother's milk. Six in the morning, twelve noon, six in the evening and midnight is about the best schedule since it fits in with most human eating plans. Meals for the puppies can be prepared immediately before or after your own meals, without too much of a change in your schedule.

6 A.M.

Two meat and two milk meals serve best and should be served alternately, of course. Assuming the 6 a.m. feeding is a milk meal the contents should be as follows: Goat's milk is the very best milk to feed puppies, but is expensive and usually available only at drug stores, unless you live in farm country where it could be inexpensive. If goat's milk is,not available, use evaporated milk (which can be changed to powdered milk later on) diluted to two parts evaporated milk and one part water, along with raw egg yoke, honey or Karo syrup, sprinkled with a high-protein baby cereal and some wheat germ. As the puppies mature cottage cheese may be added or, at one of the two milk meals, it can be substituted for the cereal.

NOON

A puppy chow which has been soaked according to the time specified on the wrapper should be mixed with raw or simmered chop meat in equal proportions with a vitamin powder added.

6 P.M.

Repeat the milk meal.

MIDNIGHT

Repeat the meat meal.

Please note that specific proportions of the suggested diet are not given. Each serving will depend entirely upon the size of the litter and will increase proportionately with their rate of growth. However, it is safe to say that the most important ingredients are the milk and cereal, and the meat and puppy chow which forms the basis of the diet. Your veterinarian can advise on the proportions if there is any doubt in your mind as to how much to use.

We would like to point out that there are some basic concepts in a successful feeding program. Remember, that if there is any doubt in your mind about an ingredient, ask yourself, "Would I give it to my own baby?" If the answer is no, then don't give it to your puppies. At this age, the comparison between puppies and human babies can be a good guide.

If you notice that the puppies are "cleaning their plates" you are perhaps not feeding enough to keep up with their rate of growth. Increase the amount at the next feeding. Observe them closely; puppies should each "have their fill" because their rate of growth is so rapid at this age. If they have not satisfied themselves, increase your proportions for the next feeding. You will find that if given all they can handle, they will not overeat. When they know they do not have to fight for the last morsel, they will eat to their natural capacity.

While it is not the most pleasant subject to discuss, many

puppies will regurgitate their food, perhaps a couple of times, before they manage to retain it. If they do bring up their food, allow them to eat it again, rather than clean it away. Sometimes additional saliva is necessary for them to digest it, and you do not want them to skip a meal because it is an unpleasant sight for you to observe.

This same regurgitation process holds true sometimes with the bitch, who will bring up her own food for her puppies every now and then. This is a natural instinct on her part which stems from the days when dogs were giving birth in the wilds. The only food the mother could provide at weaning time was too rough and indigestible for her puppies. Therefore, she took it upon herself to pre-digest the food until it could be retained by her young. Bitches today will sometimes resort to this instinct, especially bitches which love having litters and have a strong maternal instinct. Some help you wean their litters, others give up feeding entirely once they see you are taking over.

Winner of the Old English Sheepdog Specialty Show in Rye, New York on September 19, 1951 was Champion December Snow.

Waiting for the postman. Lady Myra and Lady Celina of Infield Hut live on a farm in Honey Brook, Pennsylvania and are co-owned by S. Clofine, M. Lerner, and R. Jutes.

When weaning the mother is kept away from the puppies for longer and longer periods of time. This is done over a period of several days. Then she is eventually separated from them all day, leaving her with them only at night for comfort and warmth. This gradual separation aids in helping the mother's milk disappear gradually and her suffering less distress after feeding a large litter.

If the mother continues to carry a great deal of milk with no signs of it tapering off, consult your veterinarian before she gets too uncomfortable. She may cut the puppies off from her supply of milk too abruptly, before they are completely on their own.

There are many opinions on the proper age to start weaning puppies. If you plan to start selling them between six and eight weeks, weaning should begin between two and three weeks of age. Here again, each bitch will pose a different problem. The size and weight of the litter should help determine this age and your veterinarian will have an opinion as he determines the burden the bitch is carrying by the size of the litter and her general condition. If she is being pulled down by feeding a large litter, he may suggest that you start at two weeks. If she is glorying in her motherhood without any apparent taxing of her strength he may suggest three to four weeks. You and he will be the best judges. But remember, there is no substitute that is as perfect as mother's milk—and the longer the puppies benefit from it, the better. Other food yes, but mother's milk first and foremost for the best puppies!

SOCIALIZING YOUR PUPPY

The need for puppies to get out among people and other animals cannot be stressed enough. Kennel-reared dogs are subject to all sorts of idiosyncrasies and seldom make good house dogs or normal members of the world around them when they grow up.

The crucial age, which determines the personality and general behavior patterns which will predominate the rest of the dog's life are formed between the ages of three to ten weeks. This is particularly true during the 21st to 28th day. It is essential that the puppy be socialized during this time by bringing him into the family life as much as possible. Floor surfaces, indoor and outdoor, should be experienced; handling by all members of the family and visitors is important, as is preliminary grooming; light training, such as setting him up on tables and cleaning teeth and ears and cutting nails, etc., has to be started early if he is to become a show dog. The puppy should be exposed to car riding, shopping tours, a leash around its neck, children—your own and others, and in all possible ways develop relationships with humans.

It is up to the breeder, of course, to protect the puppy from harm or injury during this initiation into the wide world. The benefits reaped from proper attention will pay off in the long run with a well-behaved, well-adjusted grown dog capable of becoming an integral part of a happy family.

CHAPTER 10

TRAINING YOUR OLD ENGLISH SHEEPDOG

There are few things in the world a dog would rather do than please his master. Therefore, obedience training, or even the initial basic training, will be a pleasure for your dog, if taught correctly, and will make him a much nicer animal to live with for the rest of his life.

WHEN TO START TRAINING

The most frequently asked question by those who consider training their dog is, naturally, "What is the best age to begin training?" The answer is, "not before six months." A dog simply cannot be sufficiently or permanently trained before this age and be expected to retain all he has been taught. If too much is expected of him, he can become frustrated and it may ruin him completely for any serious training later on, or even jeopardize his disposition. Most things a puppy learns and repeats before he is six months of age should be considered habit rather than training.

THE REWARD METHOD

The only proper and acceptable kind of training is the kindness and reward method which will build a strong bond between dog and owner. A dog must have confidence in and respect for his teacher. The most important thing to remember in training any dog is that the quickest way to teach, especially the young dog, is through repetition. Praise him when he does well, and scold him when he does wrong. This will suffice. There is no need or excuse for swinging at a dog with rolled up newspapers, or flailing hands which will only tend to make the dog hand shy the rest of his life. Also, make every word count. Do not give a command unless you intend to see it through. Pronounce distinctly with the fewest possible words, and use the same words for the same command every time.

Include the dog's name every time to make sure you have his undivided attention at the beginning of each command. Do not go on to another command until he has successfully completed the previous one and is praised for it. Of course, you should not mix play with the serious training time. Make sure the dog knows the difference between the two.

In the beginning, it is best to train without any distractions whatsoever. After he has learned to concentrate and is older and more proficient, be should perform the exercises with interference, so that the dog learns absolute obedience in the face of all distractions. Needless to say, whatever the distractions, you never lose control. You must be in command at all times to earn the respect and attention of your dog.

HOW LONG SHOULD THE LESSONS BE?

The lessons should be brief with a young dog, starting at five minutes, and as the dog ages and becomes adept in the first lessons,

A working dog at work! Photo by Percy T. Jones.

Ch. Ragbears Hair Apparent gives his handler Dick Baum a big wet kiss after their most recent win. Owner/breeder Gail Fletcher of Tucson, Arizona stands by. Photo by Jayne Langdon.

increase the time all the way up to one-half hour. Public training classes are usually set for one hour, and this is acceptable since the full hour of concentration is not placed on your dog alone. Working under these conditions with other dogs, you will find that he will not be as intent as he would be with a private lesson where the commands are directed to him alone for the entire thirty minutes.

If you should notice that your dog is not doing well, or not keeping up with the class, consider putting off training for awhile. Animals, like children, are not always ready for schooling at exactly the same age. It would be a shame to ruin a good obedience dog because you insist on starting his training at six months rather than at, say, nine months, when he would be more apt to be receptive both physically and mentally. If he has particular difficulty in learning one exercise, you might do well to skip to a different one and come back to it again at another session. There are no set rules in this basic training, except, "don't push"!

WHAT YOU NEED TO START TRAINING

From three to six months of age, use the soft nylon show leads, which are the best and safest. When you get ready for the basic training at six months of age, you will require one of the special metal-link choke chains sold for exactly this purpose. Do not let the word "choke" scare you. It is a soft, smooth chain and should be held slack whenever you are not actually using it to correct the dog. This chain should be put over the dog's head so that the lead can be attached over the dog's neck rather than underneath against his throat. It is wise when you buy your choke collar to ask the sales person to show you how it is to be put on. Those of you who will be taking your dog to a training class will have an instructor who can show you.

To avoid undue stress on the dog, use both hands on the lead. The dog will be taught to obey commands at your left side, and therefore, your left hand will guide the dog close to this collar on a six-foot training lead. The balance of the lead will be held in your right hand. Learn at the very beginning to handle your choke collar and lead correctly. It is as important in training a dog as is the proper equipment for riding a horse.

WHAT TO TEACH FIRST

The first training actually should be to teach the dog to know his name. This, of course, he can learn at an earlier age than six months, just as he can learn to walk nicely on a leash or lead. Many puppies will at first probably want to walk around with the leash in their mouths. There is no objection to this if the dog will walk while doing it. Rather than cultivating this as a habit, you will find that if

Typical, adorable Old English Sheepdog . . . Lady Penelope of Infield Hut. A true herder, and her owner claims she is happy on land or on sea. So far Lady Penelope has whelped two litters, one with twelve puppies and one with nine. Owner is Steven Clofine of Divine Light Farms, Bernville, Pennsylvania.

A Working Group win for Dr. George R. Wiseman, Jr.'s Merriedip Bob-A-Long at the Toledo show several years ago. The judge is Glen Staines, the handler Billy Lang.

you don't make an issue of it, the dog will soon realize that carrying the lead in his mouth is not rewarding and he'll let it fall to his side where it belongs.

We also let the puppy walk around by himself for a while with the lead around his neck. If he wishes to chew on it a little, that's all right too. In other words, let it be something he recognizes and associates with at first. Do not let the lead start out being a harness.

If the dog is at all bright, chances are he has learned to come on command when you call him by name. This is relatively simple with sweet talk and a reward. On lead, without a reward, and on command without a lead is something else again. If there has been, or is now, a problem, the best way to correct it is to put on the choke collar and the six-foot lead. Then walk away from the dog, and call him, "Pirate, come!" and gently start reeling him in until the dog is in front of you. Give him a pat on the head and/or a reward.

Walking, or heeling, next to you is also one of the first and most important things for him to learn. With the soft lead training starting very early, he should soon take up your pace at your left side. At the command to "heel" he should start off with you and continue alongside until you stop. Give the command, "Pirate, sit!"

This is taught by leaning over and pushing down on his hindquarters until he sits next to you, while pulling up gently on the collar. When you have this down pat on the straight away, then start practicing it in circles, with turns and figure eights. When he is an advanced student, you can look forward to the heels and sits being done neatly, spontaneously, and off lead as well.

THE "DOWN" COMMAND

One of the most valuable lessons or commands you can teach your dog is to lie down on command. Some day it may save his life, and is invaluable when traveling with a dog or visiting, if behavior and manners are required even beyond obedience. While repeating the words, "Pirate, down!" lower the dog from a sitting position in front of you by gently pulling his front legs out in front of him. Place your full hand on him while repeating the command, "Pirate, down!" and hold him down to let him know you want him to *stay* down. After he gets the general idea, this can be done from a short distance away on lead along with the command, by pulling the lead down to the floor. Or perhaps, you can slip the lead under your shoe (between the heel and the sole) and pull it directly to the floor. As the dog progresses in training, a hand signal with or without verbal command, or with or without lead, can be given from a considerable distance by raising your arm and extending the hand palm down.

THE "STAY" COMMAND

The stay command eventually can be taught from both a sit and a down position. Start with the sit. With your dog on your left side in the sitting position give the command, "Pirate, stay!" Reach down with the left hand open and palm side to the dog and sweep it in close to his nose. Then walk a short distance away and face him. He will at first, having learned to heel immediately as you start off, more than likely start off with you. The trick in teaching this is to make sure he hears "stay" before you start off. It will take practice.

Champion Shagbourne Monarch, Best In Show, pictured with owner Hazel Liptak of Plymouth, Michigan. The judge was Mr. A. W. Brockway and the show was the 1950 Muskegon-Grand Haven Kennel Club. Photograph courtesy of the *Muskegon Chronicle.*

My Own Miss Whiskers, owned by Erna M. Haurin, photographed many years ago.

Ch. Rollingsea Emperor, the English import owned and shown by the Marvin Smiths, Tamara Kennels, Brighton, Michigan. This picture was taken when he was 16 months old, and finishing toward his American championship.

If he breaks, sit him down again, stand next to him, and give the command all over again. As he masters the command, let the distance between you and your dog increase while the dog remains seated. Once the command is learned, advance to the stay command from the down position.

THE STAND FOR EXAMINATION

If you have any intention of going on to advanced training in obedience with your dog, or if you have a show dog which you feel you will enjoy showing yourself, a most important command which should be mastered at six months of age, is the stand command. This is essential for a show dog since it is the position used when the show judge goes over your dog. This is taught in the same manner as the stay command, but this time with the dog remaining up on all four feet. He should learn to stand still, without moving his feet and without flinching or breaking when approached by either you or strangers. The hand with palm open wide and facing him

The 1952 Old English Sheepdog Club of America Specialty, held in Port Chester, New York, in June of that year, saw judge Dr. J. P. McCain place Herbert Gilg's Ch. Marbert Highland Tuffy Best of Breed and Barclay Acheson's Shepton Blushing Maid Best of Opposite Sex. Both dogs were owner-handled to these impressive wins.

The 1950 Cheyenne Kennel Club on June 25th found judge Major Bryant Godsol awarding Best In Show to N. G. Smith's Ch. Lynnhaven Great Son. Judge Godsol also gave the dog Best of Breed, and Mrs. Beatrice Godsol gave him the Working Group on his way to Best In Show.

should be firmly placed in front of his nose with the command, "Pirate, stand!" After he learns the basic rules and knows the difference between stand and stay, ask friends, relatives, and strangers to assist you with this exercise by walking up to the dog and going over him. He should not react physically to their touch. A dog posing in this stance should show all the beauty and pride of being a sterling example of his breed.

FORMAL SCHOOL TRAINING

We mentioned previously about the various training schools and classes given for dogs. Your local kennel club, newspaper, or the yellow pages of the telephone book will put you in touch with organizations in your area where this service is performed. You and your dog will learn a great deal from these classes. Not only do they offer formal training, but the experience for you and your dog in public, with other dogs of approximately the same age and with the

Above and opposite: the **Old English Sheepdog** in action! The camera of Don Ashman captures Beau Chevals Sir Lancelot as he leaps and bounds over the property of his owners, Mr. and Mrs. Edward Beegle of Holicong, Pennsylvania. Lance, as he is known to his owners, is a true working dog.

Training for the show ring! Kimberly Violante and her Beau Cheval Old English Sheepdog start training early in York, Pennsylvania.

same purpose in mind is invaluable. If you intend to show your dog, this training is valuable ring experience for later on. If you are having difficulty with the training, remember, it is either too soon to start—or YOU are doing something wrong!

ADVANCED TRAINING AND OBEDIENCE TRIALS

The A.K.C. obedience trials are divided into three classes: Novice, Open and Utility.

In the Novice Class, the dog will be judged on the following basis:

TEST	MAXIMUM SCORE
Heel on lead	35
Stand for examination	30
Heel free—on lead	45
Recall (come on command)	30
One-minute sit (handler in ring)	30
Three-minute down (handler in ring)	30
Maximum total score	200

If the dog "qualifies" in three shows by earning at least 50% of the points for each test, with a total of at least 170 for the trial, he has earned the Companion Dog degree and the letters C.D. (Companion Dog) are entered after his name in the A.K.C. records.

After the dog has qualified as a C.D., he is eligible to enter the Open Class competition, where he will be judged on this basis:

TEST	MAXIMUM SCORE
Heel free	40
Drop on Recall	30
Retrieve (wooden dumbbell) on flat	25
Retrieve over obstacle (hurdle)	35
Broad jump	20
Three-minute sit (handler out of ring)	25
Five-minute down (handler out of ring)	25
Maximum total score	200

Again he must qualify in three shows for the C.D.X. (Companion Dog Excellent) title and then is eligible for the Utility Class, where he can earn the Utility Dog (U.D.) degree in these rugged tests:

TEST	MAXIMUM SCORE
Scent discrimination (picking up article handled by master from group) Article 1	20
Scent discrimination Article 2	20
Scent discrimination Article 3	20
Seek back (picking up an article dropped by handler)	30
Signal exercise (heeling, etc., on hand signal)	35
Directed jumping (over hurdle and bar jump)	40
Group examination	35
Maximum total score	200

For more complete information about these obedience trials, write for the American Kennel Club's *Regulations and Standards for Obedience Trials*. Dogs that are disqualified from breed shows because of alteration or physical defects are eligible to compete in these trials.

CHAPTER 11

SHOWING YOUR OLD ENGLISH SHEEPDOG

Let us assume that after a few months of tender loving care, you realize your dog is developing beyond your wildest expectations and that the dog you selected is very definitely a show dog! Of course, every owner is prejudiced. But if you are sincerely interested in going to dog shows with your dog and making a champion of him, now is the time to start casting a critical eye on him from a judge's point of view.

There is no such thing as a perfect dog. Every dog has some faults perhaps even a few serious ones. The best way to appraise your dog's degree of perfection is to compare him with the Standard for the breed, or before a judge in a show ring.

MATCH SHOWS

For the beginner there are "mock" dog shows, called Match Shows, where you and your dog go through many of the procedures of a regular dog show, but do not gain points toward championship. These shows are usually held by kennel clubs, annually or semi-annually, and much ring poise and experience can be gained there. The age limit is reduced to two months at match shows to give puppies four months of training before they compete at the regular shows when they reach six months of age. Classes range from two to four months; four to six months; six to nine months; and nine to twelve months. Puppies compete with others of their own age for comparative purposes. Many breeders evaluate their litters in this manner, choosing which is the most outgoing, which is the most poised, the best showman, etc.

For those seriously interested in showing their dog to full championship, these match shows provide important experience for both the dog and the owner. Class categories may vary slightly, according to number of entries, but basically include all the classes that are included at a regular point show. There is a nominal entry fee and, of course, ribbons and usually trophies are given for your efforts as well. Unlike the point shows, entries can be made on the day of the show right on the show grounds. They are unbenched and provide an informal, usually congenial atmosphere for the amateur, which helps to make the ordeal of one's first adventures in the show ring a little less nerve-wracking.

THE POINT SHOWS

It is not possible to show a puppy at an American Kennel Club sanctioned point show before the age of six months. When your dog reaches this eligible age, your local kennel club can provide you with the names and addresses of the show-giving superintendents in your area who will be staging the club's dog show for them, and where you must write for an entry form. A sample entry form is included in this book.

The forms are mailed in a pamphlet called a premium list. This also includes the names of the judges for each breed, a list of the prizes and trophies, the name and address of the show-giving club and where the show will be held, as well as rules and regulations set up by the American Kennel Club which must be abided by if you are to enter.

A booklet containing the complete set of show rules and regulations may be obtained by writing to the American Kennel Club, Inc., 51 Madison Avenue, New York, N.Y., 10010.

When you write to the Dog Show Superintendent, request not only your premium list for this particular show, but ask that your name be added to their mailing list so that you will automatically receive all premium lists in the future. List your breed or breeds and they will see to it that you receive premium lists for Specialty shows as well.

Unlike the match shows where your dog will be judged on ring behavior, at the point shows he will be judged on conformation to the breed Standard. In addition to being at least six months of age (on the day of the show) he must be a thoroughbred for a point show. This means both of his parents and he are registered with the American Kennel Club. There must be no alterations or falsifications regarding his appearance. Females cannot have been spayed and males must have both testicles in evidence. No dyes or

The well-known Old English Sheepdog fancier Mrs. C. M. Crafts pictured at a dog show with one of her lovely puppies.

A charming informal photograph taken by Edwin Levick at the Lenox Dog Show several years ago captures the likenesses of Mrs. Wayne Heffner of Phoenix, Arizona and Mrs. Arnold of New York City sitting with Mrs. Lewis Roesler (center) and some of her Old English Sheepdog puppies. Photo by Edwin Levick.

powders may be used to enhance the appearance, and any lameness or deformity or major deviation from the Standard for the breed constitutes a disqualification.

With all these things in mind, groom your dog to the best of your ability in the specified area for this purpose in the show hall and walk into the show ring with great pride of ownership and ready for an appraisal of your dog by the judge.

The presiding judge on that day will allow each and every dog a certain amount of time and consideration before making his

Ch. Paul of Square Four, owned by Barclay Acheson of Briarcliff Manor, New York, wins Best In Show under judge Carlos L. Henriquez, Jr. at the Sewickley Valley Kennel Association show in September, 1952. Handler is E. J. Carver. Photo by Norton of Kent.

The Old English Sheepdog Club of America Specialty Show held on June 6, 1959, saw Ch. Shepton Bridewell Bo-Peep go Best of Opposite Sex. Bo-Peep is owned by the Waterfall Kennels. James Trullinger was the judge, with Ed Carver handling for the owner. Photo by Brown.

decisions. It is never permissible to consult the judge regarding either your dog or his decision while you are in the ring. An exhibitor never speaks unless spoken to, and then only to answer such questions as the judge may ask—the age of the dog, the dog's bite, or to ask you to move your dog around the ring once again.

However, before you reach the point where you are actually in the ring awaiting the final decisions of the judge, you will have had to decide on which of the five classes in each sex your dog should compete.

Ch. Kings Messenger, owned by Lt. Stanley F. Kraft of Cleveland, Ohio, is pictured after winning Working Group.

The famous and fabulous Ch. Merriedip Duke George, one of the top-winning Old English Sheepdogs in the breed. He was owned by Mrs. Mona Berkowitz of California.

Ch. Rosmoore Smarty Pants receives the presentation of the prize for his owner, Mrs. C. M. Crafts, for best American-bred dog bred by the exhibitor, presented by Percy Roberts at the annual members' match show of the New England Old English Sheepdog Club; the show was held in Great Barrington, Massachusetts in August, 1941.

Champion Lillibrad Prince Charming, owned by Mr. A. V. Gustafson of Chicago, Illinois, captures the coveted Best In Show win under judge Percy Roberts at the Kankakee Kennel Club show in July, 1960. Handled by Jack Funk, this was just one of Prince Charming's Top show awards. Frasie photo.

←

Another Best In Show Old English Sheepdog which did a lot of winning in the 1950's: Ch. Norval Pride, owned by B. H. and Lillian Lovejoy of Denver, Colorado. Here he is pictured winning Best In Show under judge McQuoen at the 52nd Fall show of the Colorado Kennel Club.

Point Show Classes

The regular classes of the AKC are: Puppy, Novice, Bred-by-Exhibitor, American-Bred, Open; if your dog is undefeated in any of the regular classes (divided by sex) in which it is entered, he or she is **required** to enter the Winners Class. If your dog is placed second in the class to the dog which won Winners Dog or Winners Bitch, hold the dog or bitch in readiness as the judge must consider it for Reserve Winners.

Puppy Classes shall be for dogs which are six months of age and over but under twelve months, which were whelped in the U.S.A. or Canada, and which are not champions. Classes are often divided 6 and (under) 9, and 9 and (under) 12 months. The age of a dog shall be calculated up to and inclusive of the first day of a show. For example, a dog whelped on Jan. 1st is eligible to compete in a puppy class on July 1st, and may continue to compete up to and including Dec. 31st of the same year, but is not eligible to compete Jan. 1st of the following year.

The Novice Class shall be for dogs six months of age or over, whelped in the U.S.A. or Canada which have not, prior to the closing of entries, won three first prizes in the Novice Class, a first prize in Bred-by-Exhibitor, American-Bred or Open Class, nor one or more points toward a championship title.

The Bred-by-Exhibitor Class shall be for dogs whelped in the U.S.A. which are six months of age and over, which are not champions, and which are owned wholly or in part by the person or by the spouse of the person who was the breeder or one of the breeders of record. Dogs entered in the BBE Class must be handled by an owner or by a member of the immediate family of an owner, i.e., the husband, wife, father, mother, son, daughter, brother or sister.

The American-Bred Class shall be for all dogs (except champions) six months of age or over, whelped in the U.S.A. by reason of a mating that took place in the U.S.A.

The Open Class is for any dog six months of age or over, except in a member specialty club show held for only American-Bred dogs, in which case the class is for American-Bred dogs only.

Winners Dogs and **Winners Bitches:** After the above male classes have been judged, the first-place winners are then **required**

Merriedip Master Pantaloons, a Best In Show winner, displays another of his many talents . . . guardian of the home!

Shepton Blue Prince of Round Table tops the Working Group at the 1941 show for the Berks Country Kennel Club held in Reading, Pa. Dr. Louis Cornet was the judge, James McNaull was the handler for Prince, and Mrs. John Springer was the steward. Photo by Percy T. Jones.

to compete in the ring. The dog judged "Winners Dog" is awarded the points toward his championship title.

Reserve Winners are selected immediately after the Winners Dog. In case of a disqualification of a win by the AKC, the Reserve Dog moves up to "Winners" and receives the points. After all male classes are judged, the bitch classes are called.

Best of Breed or Best of Variety Competition is limited to Champions of Record or dogs (with newly acquired points, for a 90-day period prior to AKC confirmation) which have completed championship requirements, and Winners Dog and Winners Bitch (or the dog awarded Winners if only one Winners prize has been awarded), together with any undefeated dogs which have been shown only in non-regular classes, all compete for Best of Breed or Best of Variety (if the breed is divided by size, color, texture or length of coat hair, etc.).

Best of Winners: If the WD or WB earns BOB or BOV, it automatically becomes BOW; otherwise they will be judged together for BOW (following BOB or BOV judging).

Best of Opposite Sex is selected from the remaining dogs of the opposite sex to Best of Breed or Best of Variety.

Other Classes may be approved by the AKC: **Stud Dogs, Brood Bitches, Brace Class, Team Class;** classes consisting of local dogs and bitches may also be included in a show if approved by the AKC (special rules are included in the AKC Rule Book).

The **Miscellaneous Class** shall be for purebred dogs of such breeds as may be designated by the AKC. No dog shall be eligible for entry in this class unless the owner has been granted an Indefinite Listing Privilege (ILP) and unless the ILP number is given on the entry form. Application for an ILP shall be made on a form provided by the AKC and when submitted must be accompanied by a fee set by the Board of Directors.

All Miscellaneous Breeds shall be shown together in a single class except that the class may be divided by sex if so specified in the premium list. There shall be **no** further competition for dogs entered in this class. Ribbons for 1st, 2nd, 3rd and 4th shall be Rose, Brown, Light Green and Gray, respectively. This class is open to the following Miscellaneous Breeds: Akitas, Australian Cattle Dogs, Australian Kelpies, Border Collies, Cavalier King Charles Spaniels, Ibizan Hounds, Miniature Bull Terriers,

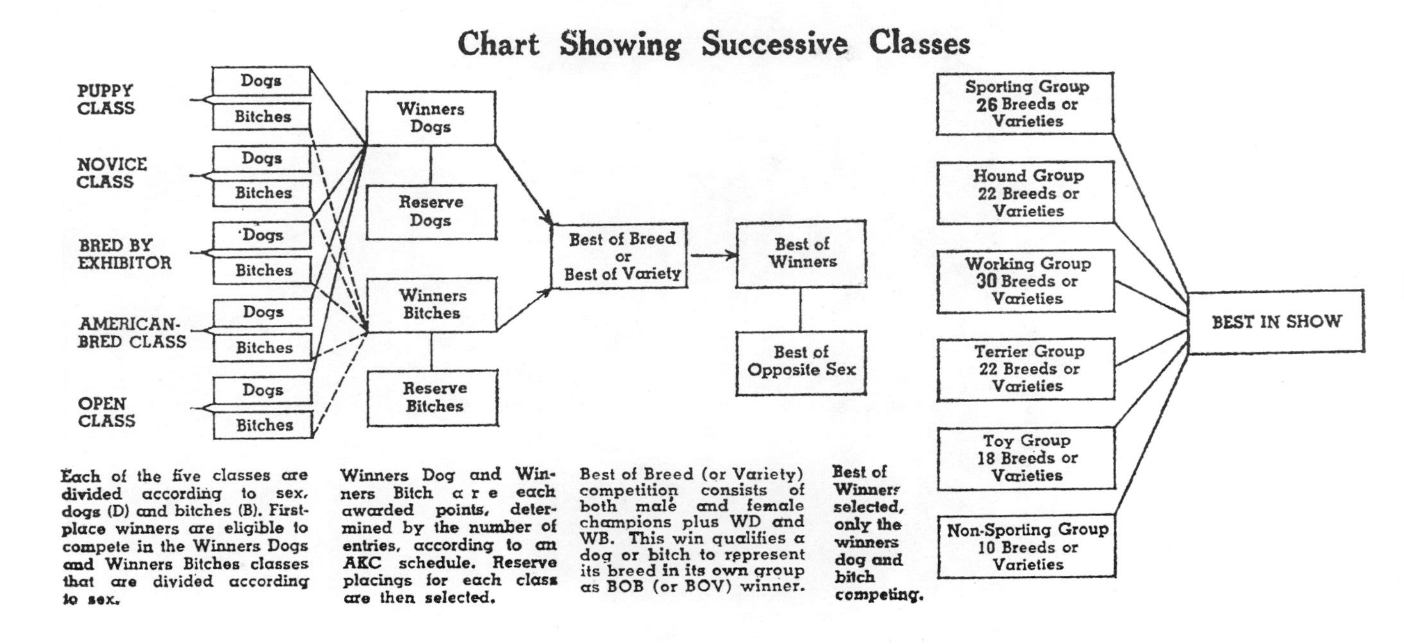
Chart Showing Successive Classes
PUPPY CLASS
NOVICE CLASS
BRED BY EXHIBITOR
AMERICAN-BRED CLASS
OPEN CLASS
Dogs
Bitches
Winners Dogs
Reserve Dogs
Winners Bitches
Reserve Bitches
Best of Breed or Best of Variety
Best of Winners
Best of Opposite Sex
Sporting Group 26 Breeds or Varieties
Hound Group 22 Breeds or Varieties
Working Group 30 Breeds or Varieties
Terrier Group 22 Breeds or Varieties
Toy Group 18 Breeds or Varieties
Non-Sporting Group 10 Breeds or Varieties
BEST IN SHOW
Each of the five classes are divided according to sex, dogs (D) and bitches (B). First-place winners are eligible to compete in the Winners Dogs and Winners Bitches classes that are divided according to sex.
Winners Dog and Winners Bitch are each awarded points, determined by the number of entries, according to an AKC schedule. Reserve placings for each class are then selected.
Best of Breed (or Variety) competition consists of both male and female champions plus WD and WB. This win qualifies a dog or bitch to represent its breed in its own group as BOB (or BOV) winner.
Best of Winners selected, only the winners dog and bitch competing.

1961 was the year, and Mrs. C. M. Crafts handled her very own Ch. Rosmoore Ole Bill to another major show win. Photo by Brown.

A photograph of classic beauty . . . Mrs. Lewis Roesler pictured with a few of her Sheepdog puppies at the Lenox dog show several years ago. Photo by Edwin Levick, New York.

This commercial photograph was part of an advertisement for cotton-cushioned innerspring mattresses and appeared in all the leading national magazines for the National Cotton Batting Institute of Memphis, Tennessee .

This picture appeared in color in an advertisement for Aileen, Inc. in the **The York Times** in October, 1972, further adding to the popularity and prestige to the Old English Sheepdog.

Beckington Happy-Go-Lucky, owned by Mrs. C. W. Chatfield, photographed in 1959.

Carol Weisbach and her one-year-old Old English, Betsy's Blue Plate Special. He is the Weisbach's family dog, and they hope a future champion. The Weisbachs live in Pennsburg, Pennsylvania.

The Beegles, of Holicong, Pennsylvania, set up this interesting Old English Sheepdog foursome for the camera during the 1940's. It is interesting to note how true to type the Bobtails were even more than a quarter of a century ago.

A Bobtail takes another Best In Show! This time it's Ch. Brooks Blue Boy, owned by Florence E. Pangborn and handled by George E. Carlton, at the Magic Valley Kennel Club show in Charleston, West Virginia in July, 1971. The judge is Mrs. Patterson and the photographer Norton of Kent.

Soft-coated Wheaten Terriers, Spinoni Italiani and Tibetan Terriers.

If Your Dog Wins a Class . . .

Study the classes to make certain your dog is entered in a proper class for his or her qualifications. If your dog wins his class, the rule states: *You are required* to enter classes for Winners, Best of Breed and Best of Winners (no additional entry fees). The rule states, "No eligible dog may be withheld from competition." It is not mandatory that you stay for group judging. If *your dog wins a group*, however, *you must stay for Best-in-Show competition.*

THE PRIZE RIBBONS AND WHAT THEY STAND FOR

No matter how many entries there are in each class at a dog show, if you place first through fourth position you will receive a ribbon.

These ribbons commemorate your win and can be impressive when collected and displayed to prospective buyers when and if you have puppies for sale, or if you intend to use your dog at public stud.

All ribbons from the American Kennel Club licensed dog shows will bear the American Kennel Club seal, the name of the show, the date and the placement. In the classes the colors are blue for first, red for second, yellow for third, and white for fourth. Winners Dog or Winners Bitch ribbons are purple, while Reserve Dog and Reserve Bitch ribbons are purple and white. Best of Winners ribbons are blue and white; Best of Breed, purple and gold; and Best of Opposite Sex ribbons are red and white.

In the six groups, first prize is a blue rosette or ribbon, second placement is red, third yellow, and fourth white. The Best In Show rosette is either red, white and blue, or incorporates the colors used in the show-giving club's emblem.

A lovely outline photograph of the Charles W. Chatfields' Happy-Go-Lucky.

OFFICIAL AMERICAN KENNEL CLUB ENTRY FORM

- - - INSERT BELOW — NAME OF CLUB and DATE OF SHOW - - -

CLUB ....

DATE ....

ENTRY FORM MUST BE SIGNED on the bottom line ● **by the owner or the owner's duly authorized agent, otherwise entry cannot be accepted.**

MAKE CHECKS payable to **Foley Dog Show Organization, Inc.**

MAIL ENTRIES with FEES to Alan P. Winks, Superintendent, 2009 Ranstead Street, Philadelphia, PA 19103.

JUNIOR SHOWMANSHIP ENTRANTS must complete both sides of this entry form.

PLEASE TYPEWRITE OR PRINT CLEARLY

I ENCLOSE $............................**for entry fees.**

● **IMPORTANT—Read Carefully Instructions on Reverse Side Before Filling Out**

Breed	**Variety** See Instruction #1, reverse side (if any)	**Sex**
DOG Show Class — See Instruction #2, reverse side (Give age, color or weight if class divided)	**Obedience Trial Class**	
If dog is entered for Best of Breed (Variety) Competition—see Instruction #3 reverse side — CHECK THIS BOX ☐	**Additional Classes**	

If entry of dog is to be made in Jr. Showmanship as well as in one of the above competitions, check this box, and fill in data on reverse side. ☐

If for Jr. Showmanship only then check THIS box, and fill in data on reverse side. ☐

Name of Actual Owner(s)	See Instruction #4, reverse side
Name of Licensed Handler (if any)	[**handler**] ●
Full Name of Dog	●
Insert one of the following: **AKC Reg. #** **AKC Litter #** **I.L.P. #** **Foreign Reg. # & Country**	**Date of Birth** — **Place of Birth** ☐ U.S.A. ☐ Canada ☐ Foreign — Do not print the above in catalog ● — **Breeder,** ●
Sire	
Dam	●

Owner's Name ______________________________
(Please print)

Owner's Address ______________________________

City ____________ **State** ____________ **Zip Code** ____________

I CERTIFY that I am the actual owner of this dog, or that I am the duly authorized agent of the actual owner whose name I have entered above. In consideration of the acceptance of this entry, I (we) agree to abide by the rules and regulations of The American Kennel Club in effect at the time of this show or obediance trial, and by any additional rules and regulations appearing in the premium list for this show or obedience trial or both, and further agree to be bound by the "Agreement" printed on the reverse side of this entry form. I (we) certify and represent that the dog entered is not a hazard to persons or other dogs. This entry is submitted for acceptance on the foregoing representation and agreement.

SIGNATURE of owner or his agent ●
duly authorized to make this entry ______________________________

Single copies of the latest editions of the "Rules Applying to Registration and Dog Shows" and "Obedience Regulations" may be obtained WITHOUT CHARGE from any Superintendent or from THE AMERICAN KENNEL CLUB, 51 MADISON AVENUE, NEW YORK, N. Y. 10010.

AGREEMENT

I (we) acknowledge that the "Rules Applying to Registration and Dog Shows" and, if this entry is for an obedience trial, the "Obedience Regulations," have been made available to me (us), and that I am (we are) familiar with their contents. I (we) agree that the club holding this show or obedience trial has the right to refuse this entry for cause which the club shall deem to be sufficient. In consideration of the acceptance of this entry and of the holding of the show or obedience trial and of the opportunity to have the dog judged and to win prize money, ribbons, or trophies, I (we) agree to hold this club, its members, directors, governors, officers, agents, superintendents or show secretary, and any employees of the aforementioned parties, harmless from any claim for loss or injury which may be alleged to have been caused directly or indirectly to any person or thing by the act of this dog while in or upon the show or obedience trial premises or grounds or near any entrance thereto, and I (we) personally assume all responsibility and liability for any such claim; and I (we) further agree to hold the aforementioned parties harmless from any claim for loss of this dog by disappearance, theft, death or otherwise, and from any claim for damage or injury to the dog, whether such loss, disappearance, theft, damage, or injury, be caused or alleged to be caused by the negligence of the club or any of the parties aforementioned, or by the negligence of any other person, or any other cause or causes.

INSTRUCTIONS

1. (Variety) If you are entering a dog of a breed in which there are varieties for show purposes, please designate the particular variety you are entering, i. e., Cocker Spaniel (solid color black, ASCOB, parti-color), Beagles (not exceeding 13 in.; over 13 in. but not exceeding 15 in.), Dachshunds (longhaired, smooth, wirehaired), Collies (rough, smooth), Bull Terriers (colored, white), Fox Terriers (smooth, wire), Manchester Terriers (standard, toy), Chihuahuas (smooth coat, long coat), English Toy Spaniels (King Charles and Ruby, Blenheim and Prince Charles), Poodles (toy, miniature, standard).
2. (Dog Show Class) Consult the classification in this premium list. If the dog show class in which you are entering your dog is divided, then, in addition to designating the class, specify the particular division of the class in which you are entering your dog, i. e., age division, color division, weight division.
3. The following categories of dogs may be entered and shown in Best of Breed competition: Dogs that are Champions of Record and dogs which, according to their owners' records, have completed the requirements for a championship, but whose championships are unconfirmed. The showing of unconfirmed Champions in Best of Breed competition is limited to a period of 90 days from the date of the show where the dog completed the requirements for a championship.
4. A dog must be entered in the name of the person who actually owned it at the time entries for a show closed. If a registered dog has been acquired by a new owner it must be entered in the name of its new owner in any show for which entries closed after the date of acquirement, regardless of whether the new owner has received the registration certificate indicating that the dog is recorded in his name. State on entry form whether transfer application has been mailed to A.K.C. (For complete rule refer to Chapter 16, Section 3.)

***JUNIOR SHOWMANSHIP* — If the dog identified on the front of this entry form is entered in Junior Showmanship, please give the following information:**

CLASS SEE DESCRIPTION OF JUNIOR SHOWMANSHIP CLASSES IN THIS PREMIUM LIST.

NAME OF JUNIOR HANDLER | DATE OF BIRTH

ADDRESS

CITY | STATE | ZIP CODE

If Junior Handler is not the owner of the dog identified on the face of this form, what is the relationship of the Junior Handler to the owner?

QUALIFYING FOR CHAMPIONSHIP

Championship points are given for Winners Dog and Winners Bitch in accordance with a scale of points established by the American Kennel Club based on the popularity of the breed in entries, and the number of dogs competing in the classes. This scale of points varies in different sections of the country, but the scale is published in the front of each dog show catalog. These points may differ between the dogs and the bitches at the same show. You may, however, win additional points by winning Best of Winners, if there are fewer dogs than bitches entered, or vice versa. Points never exceed five at any one show, and a total of fifteen points must be won to constitute a championship. These fifteen points must be

Best of Breed at one of the Old English Sheepdog Club Specialties was Ch. Cartref Toggery, owned by the Waterfall Kennels of Ridgefield, Connecticut. Mr. Alf Loveredge was the judge.

Ch. Bobtail Ole Blue, owned by Biaggio and Kathleen Parma of Newark, Delaware. Ole Blue was sired by Ch. Rivermist Galahad ex Ch. Bobtail Penny Paula and is handled here by Mr. Parma. A William P. Gilbert photograph.

won under at least three different judges, and you must acquire at least two major wins. Anything from a three to five point win is a major, while one and two point wins are minor wins. Two major wins must be won under two different judges to meet championship requirements.

OBEDIENCE TRIALS

Some shows also offer Obedience Trials which are considered as separate events. They give the dogs a chance to compete and score on performing a prescribed set of exercises intended to display their training in doing useful work.

There are three obedience titles for which they may compete. First, the Companion Dog or CD title; second, the Companion Dog Excellent or CDX; and third, the Utility Dog or UD. Detailed information on these degrees is contained in a booklet entitled Official Obedience Regulations and may be obtained by writing to the American Kennel Club.

JUNIOR SHOWMANSHIP COMPETITION

Junior Showmanship Competition is for boys and girls in different age groups handling their own dog or one owned by their immediate family. There are four divisions: Novice A, for the ten to 12 year olds; Novice B, for those 13 to 16 years of age, with no previous junior showmanship wins; Open C, for ten to 12 year olds; and Open D, for 13 to 16 year olds who have earned one or more JS awards.

As Junior Showmanship at the dog shows increased in popularity, certain changes and improvements had to be made. As of April 1, 1971, the American Kennel Club issued a new booklet containing the Regulations for Junior Showmanship which may be obtained by writing to the A.K.C. at 51 Madison Avenue, New York, N.Y. 10010.

DOG SHOW PHOTOGRAPHERS

Every show has at least one official photographer who will be more than happy to take a photograph of your dog with the judge, ribbons and trophies, along with you or your handler. These make marvelous remembrances of your top show wins and are frequently framed along with the ribbons for display purposes. Photographers can be paged at the show over the public address system, if you wish to obtain this service. Prices vary, but you will probably find it costs little to capture these happy moments, and the photos can always be used in the various dog magazines to advertise your dog's wins.

Ch. Ragbears Heathcliff Mist, with breeder-owner Gail Fletcher of Tucson, Arizona. This win, at the Del Monte Kennel Club show in May, 1971, was under judge Derek Rayne. Photo by Missy Yuhl.

"Duffy is the name—Stud is the Game," says American and Canadian Champion Tamara's Shaggy Shoes MacDuff, owned by Don and Jean McColl of Birmingham, Michigan.

TWO TYPES OF DOG SHOWS

There are two types of dog shows licensed by the American Kennel Club. One is the all-breed show which includes classes for all the recognized breeds, and groups of breeds; i.e., all terriers, all toys, etc. Then there are the Specialty shows for one particular breed which also offer championship points.

BENCHED OR UNBENCHED DOG SHOWS

The show-giving clubs determine, usually on the basis of what facilities are offered by their chosen show site, whether their show will be benched or unbenched. A benched show is one where the dog show superintendent supplies benches (cages for toy dogs). Each bench is numbered and its corresponding number appears on your entry identification slip which is sent to you prior to the show date. The number also appears in the show catalog. Upon entering the show you should take your dog to the bench where he should remain until it is time to groom him before entering the ring to be judged. After judging, he must be returned to the bench until the official time of dismissal from the show. At an unbenched show the club makes no provision whatsoever for your dog other than an enormous tent (if an outdoor show) or an area in a show hall where all crates and grooming equipment must be kept.

Benched or unbenched, the moment you enter the show grounds you are expected to look after your dog and have it under complete control at all times. This means short leads in crowded aisles or getting out of cars. In the case of a benched show, a "bench chain" is needed. It should allow the dog to move around, but not get

Tamara's Shaggy Heather, a daughter of Prince Charming, and owned by the Tamara Kennels, Brighton, Michigan.

down off the bench. It is also not considered "cute" to have small tots leading enormous dogs around a dog show where the child might be dragged into the middle of a dog fight.

PROFESSIONAL HANDLERS

If you are new in the fancy and do not know how to handle your dog to his best advantage, or if you are too nervous or physically

Ch. Droverdale Brother's Keeper, owned by Sue and Dana Banghart, was sired by Ch. Duke of Brunswick out of Ch. Droverdale BB Derry Aire. Brother finished at 14 months of age. Olson photo.

American and Canadian Ch. Blandford's Adebar, pictured going Best of Breed at the 1972 Canadian National Sportsmen's Dog Show, under the respected judge Alva M. Rosenberg. Adebar is owned by Agnes and Pat Miller, Blandford Kennels, Imlay City, Michigan.

unable to show your dog, you can hire a licensed professional handler who will do it for you for a specified fee. The more successful or well-known handlers charge slightly higher rates, but generally speaking there is a pretty uniform charge for this service. As the dog progresses with his wins in the show ring, the fee increases proportionately. Included in this service is professional advice on when and where to show your dog, grooming, a statement of your wins at each show, and all trophies and ribbons that the dog accumulates. Any cash award is kept by the handler as a sort of "bonus."

When engaging a handler, it is advisable to select one that does not take more dogs to a show than he can properly and comfortably

An Old English Sheepdog puppy poses at the typewriter to help publicize a benefit luncheon and fashion show for the Pennsylvania S.P.C.A. Old English Sheepdogs are frequently used in commercial advertising since they are clowns at heart and so photogenic.

handle. You want your dog to receive his individual attention and not be rushed into the ring at the last moment, because the handler has been busy with too many other dogs in other rings. Some handlers require that you deliver the dog to their establishment a few days ahead of the show so they have ample time to groom and train him. Others will accept well-behaved and previously trained and groomed dogs at ringside, if they are familiar with the dog and the owner. This should be determined well in advance of the show date. NEVER expect a handler to accept a dog at ringside that is not groomed to perfection!

There are several sources for locating a professional handler. Dog magazines carry their classified advertising; a note or telephone call to the American Kennel Club will put you in touch with several in your area. Usually, you will be billed after the day of the show.

DO YOU REALLY NEED A HANDLER?

The answer to the above question is sometimes yes! However, the answer most exhibitors give is, "But I can't *afford* a professional handler!" or, "I want to show my dog myself. Does that mean my dog will never do any big winning?"

Do you *really* need a handler to win? If you are mishandling a good dog that should be winning and isn't, because it is made to

Best In Show at the Ravenna, Ohio, Kennel Club Show in 1950 under judge John T. Marvin was Ch. December Snow, owned by William T. Houston of Mercer, Pa. Handler is Charles Meyer.

look simply terrible in the ring by its owner, the answer is yes. If you don't know how to handle a dog properly, why make your dog look bad when a handler could show it to its best advantage?

Some owners simply cannot handle a dog well and still wonder why their dogs aren't winning in the ring, no matter how hard they try. Others are nervous and this nervousness travels down the leash to the dog and the dog behaves accordingly. Some people are extroverts by nature, and these are the people who usually make excellent handlers. Of course, the biggest winning dogs at the shows usually have a lot of "show off" in their nature, too, and this helps a great deal.

Lillian Lovejoy of Denver Colorado handled her dog, Ch. Norval Pride King, to a first in the Working Group at the Nebraska Kennel Club. Judge is Alva Rosenberg.

Another Droverdale Bobtail takes a Group First. This win came under judge Heywood Hartley at the Tulsa, Oklahoma show in November, 1970. Owners Pat and Sandi Baker of Oxon Hill, Maryland.

A charming informal shot by the Frasie Studios of Best In Show dog Umm-pa's Surprise Snowfall, owned by Mrs. Cyrus Carey of Cincinnati, Ohio.

THE COST OF CAMPAIGNING A DOG WITH A HANDLER

Many champions are shown an average of 25 times before completing a championship. In entry fees at today's prices, that adds up to about $200. This does not include motel bills, traveling expenses, or food. There have been champions finished in less shows, say five to ten shows, but this is the exception rather than the rule. When and where to show should be thought out carefully so that you can perhaps save money on entries. Here is one of the services a professional handler provides that can mean a considerable saving. Hiring a handler can save money in the long run if you just wish to make a champion. If your dog has been winning

Little Lord Lambchops, Old English puppy pictured at 8½ months of age with his handler-owner, Priscilla Yager of Somerset, New Jersey, winning Reserve Winners Dog at the Ramapo Kennel Club show in 1972. Lambchops was sired by Beau Cheval's Shango ex Beau Cheval's Snow Bunny. William P. Gilbert photo.

BEST DOG
IN
SHOW

›ther Best In Show winning Old English Sheepdog, Ch. Merriedip ›ter Pantaloons, owned by Mrs. Helen Margery Lewis of Great ›rington, Mass. Pictured left to right on this gala occasion were ›rge J. McKercher, handler for Pantaloons; David Wagstaff, ›ge; owner Mrs. Lewis; and E. B. Taylor, president of the Wild-›od Kennel Club. This memorable win was photographed by ›iam Brown at the Saratoga Springs show grounds.

Ch. Merriedip Duke George, owned by Mrs. Mona Berkowitz, went Best of Breed at the Old English Sheepdog Club of America Specialty Show in June, 1958 under judge Maxwell Riddle. Also pictured is the Best of Opposite Sex bitch, Salt Box Granny Bee, owned by Ceil Day Wood. Photo by Evelyn Shafer.

›e Best In Show winner at the 1938 Morris and Essex Kennel Club ›ow in New Jersey was Champion Ideal Weather. Mrs. Geraldine ›dge, President of the M & E Kennel Club, on whose magnificent ›ounds the show was staged each year, presents the trophy.

reserves and not taking the points and a handler can finish him in five to ten shows, you would be ahead financially. If your dog is not really top quality, the length of time it takes even a handler to finish it (depending upon competition in the area) could add up to a large amount of money.

Campaigning a show specimen that not only captures the wins in his breed but wins group and Best in Show awards gets up into the big money. To cover the nation's major shows and rack up a record as one of the top dogs in the nation usually costs an owner between ten and fifteen thousand dollars a year. This includes not only the professional handler's fees for taking the dog into the ring, but the cost of conditioning and grooming, board, advertising in the dog magazines, photographs, etc.

There is great satisfaction in winning with your own dog, especially if you have trained and cared for it yourself. With today's enormous entries at the dog shows and so many worthy dogs competing for top wins, many owners who said, "I'd rather do it myself!" and meant it, became discouraged and eventually hired a handler anyway

However, if you really are in it just for the sport, you can and should handle your own dog if you want to. You can learn the tricks by attending training classes, and you can learn a lot by carefully observing the more successful professional handlers as they perform in the ring. Model yourself after the ones that command respect as being the leaders in their profession. But, if you find you'd really rather be at ringside looking on, then do get a handler so that your worthy dog gets his deserved recognition in the ring. To own a good dog and win with it is a thrill, so good luck, no matter how you do it.

SOME TIPS FOR NEW EXHIBITORS

Since many of you Bobtail exhibitors will be new to dog shows, here are a few suggestions to make your venture into this field both enjoyable and successful.

Try to avoid last-minute rushing. Plan to arrive at the dog shows considerably ahead of the scheduled hour of judging, leaving yourself time to brush and exercise your Bobtail prior to his entry into the ring. Remember that there may be traffic delays, especially

Bear Creek Yankee Clipper, co-owned by James W. Mattern and Sue V. Schwartz. He is out of Ch. Sunnybrae Rivermist Gillian and sired by Ch. Tamara's Talisman. The Matterns are owners of the Bear Creek Old English Sheepdog Kennels in East Lansing, Michigan.

Afternoon nap. . . . Biscuit, a Beau Cheval Bobtail owned by Muriel Skidell, makes a stab at sleeping before the camera interrupted.

as you near the showgrounds, and that if you have not made allowance for this, you may find yourself late for the judging or missing it entirely.

Dress comfortably but neatly, and wear something that will provide an attractive background for your dog. Wear shoes and heels which will permit you to move the dog freely. Rubber soles are helpful at outdoor shows, where the grass may be wet and slippery. Too full a skirt will billow around your dog's head, causing him to break stride and pull back as you gait him. Pleated skirts are extremely comfortable, and so are culottes; both provide freedom without superfluous fabric.

Anchor your arm card firmly into place when you receive it as you enter the ring. If it will not stay put on your upper arm, tuck it into your belt with the number clearly visible. But do not allow it to remain on your arm if it keeps sliding down annoying both you and the dog.

Keep your dog at ringside until the remainder of the class assembles, allowing him to relax. No need to be the first one in the ring.

Ch. Beau Cheval's Lord Little Chap is pictured winning a 3-point major as Best of Winners under judge Kurt Mueller, Jr., at the 1970 Sand and Sea Kennel Club Show. Bred by Marlene J. Anderson, Chappie is owned by Ann De Matteis of New Brunswick, New Jersey. Stephen Klein photograph.

Even though you may be nervous, assume an air of calm, relaxed confidence once you are inside the ring. Show your dog with an air of pride. He will catch this attitude from you and do his best. Set the dog up calmly and carefully, but practice at home until you can do it fairly fast, as the time the judge can spend on each dog is limited and every second should be made to work to your advantage. Practice before a mirror is helpful, as this way you can see for yourself how the dog will look from where the judge will be studying him. Ascertain that his forepaws are placed correctly and properly under him so that he stands squarely.

The Old English Sheepdog Club of America Specialty Show held at Port Chester, New York on June 6, 1953, saw judge Herbert Gilg award Best of Breed to Cyrus Carey's Umm-pa's Surprise Snowfall. Best of Opposite Sex went to Fred LaCrosse with his Ch. Marksman's Bing. Photo by Evelyn Shafer.

This Best In Show Old English Sheepdog, topped all the contenders at the October, 1963 Bronx County Kennel Club show under judge Nancy Buckley. Champion Tara Woods Blue Baron was handled by Charles Meyer for owner Mrs. Adeline Isakson. Pictured left to right are Club President Mr. Sheldon Selikoff; judge Buckley; the Hon. Edward R. Koch, Honorary President; owner/handler Mrs. Isakson; and James J. Kermath, Show Chairman for the Bronx County Kennel Club. Photo by Evelyn Shafer.

Arrange your dog's hindquarters to show off good angulation. But do not make the common error of pulling them out too far behind the dog, bringing about a stretched, unnatural position from which the dog will shift at the first opportunity. Be ready to display his bite yourself, which is done quickly and expertly by slipping the lips apart as the jaws remain closed. And hold the dog's head for the judge to inspect the hindquarters. He should not be expected to wrestle with your dog.

Ch. December Snow and handler Charles Meyer take another show win, this time under judge James Trullinger at the Kanadasage Kennel Club show at Clyde, New York in October, 1950. The dog is owned by Mr. William T. Houston of Mercer, Pa., and was photographed by Christy of Ellesworth.

Listen carefully to the judge's instructions when he requests that you gait your dog, then follow them exactly. Some judges like the dogs moved in a "T"-shaped pattern; others prefer just down the ring and back, preferring to watch side action as the dogs circle the ring. In gaiting your dog, always keep the dog between yourself and the judge. Do not race your dog or string him up on so tight a lead that his forepaws barely touch the ground. Most dogs look their best gaiting at a moderate speed and should be trained to do so on a loose lead. Do not allow the dog to sidetrack, flop, or weave as you move him. He should travel in a straight line to and from the judge, as it is this way that he will be seen to best advantage. And of course you should have him trained to walk quietly on a lead even under distracting circumstances before you take him to a show. A dog that pulls and lunges at his competitors is a nuisance in the ring, disturbing the judging and ruining his own chances of being seen in a favorable light.

You will want to "bait" your dog to keep him alertly on his toes during the judging. For this some very well cooked liver is most generally used and is preferable to a squeaky toy, which will distract the other dogs. Keep the liver in your hand, either giving it to the dog or carrying it with you as you leave the ring. Do NOT drop bits of liver on the floor, where they will excite and disturb dogs that follow yours in the ring.

Assuming that you intend to handle the dog yourself, put aside a few moments of each day to work with him, going through ring routine to keep both of you in practice and on your toes. Set him up as you will for judging, teaching him to hold that pose. Teach him to walk sedately at your side. And make these practice sessions pleasant for him, rewarding good behavior with a petting and a treat.

Remember that your show dog needs exercise to keep in top condition. See that he has a good romp daily, plus a fairly brisk walk with you. He will not keep fit just sitting around a fenced-in yard. Take him with you in the car so that he will enjoy riding and not become carsick en route to the shows. Teach him to like being in a crate. This is the safest way for a dog to travel, so get him used to a crate at home by fixing a bed for him in a large, roomy one in a convenient place for him to use as headquarters. Keep him socialized and accustomed to strangers and strange dogs by taking him around with you downtown and on shopping trips. All these things will have bearing on his show career and add to the pleasure you take in your dog as well.

Champion Shaggywonder Prince Charming, sire of eight champions, four of which finished in 1972. Owned by the Marvin Smiths of Brighton, Michigan.

This exquisite livingroom setting featuring a Bobtail as a part of the family was featured nation-wide in a Kroehler Manufacturing Company advertising campaign. Kroehler Furniture is the product, and Company Executive Vice President T. L. Henderson raises Old English Sheepdogs.

Ch. Norval Pride King, owned by E. H. and Lillian Lovejoy of Denver, Colorado. Photo by H. Tepe.

CHAPTER 12

GENERAL CARE AND MANAGEMENT

HOUSING THE OLD ENGLISH SHEEPDOG

Proper kennel facilities for an Old English Sheepdog should be carefully thought out . . . certainly before you actually buy the dog. Those who have owned Sheepdogs know that they can be escape artists! We have found that a covered run, with metal or wooden sides half way up and wire the rest of the way up to a roof is about the best. Fiberglass used as roofing has been successful in many modern kennels and looks attractive as well.

The floor of the run should be filled at least two feet deep with crushed half-inch stone. Although many kennels use pea gravel or river bed gravel, we cannot recommend it. Cinder blocks placed in the excavated area first, spaced about two to four feet apart, will make it virtually impossible for the dog to dig out and will require less stone to fill. Stone affords the very best drainage and allows for easier picking up, and therefore, cleaner dogs! Dirt runs are most undesirable for Sheepdogs; cement runs stay wet and need washing down frequently in winter and summer.

There are many types of fencing available. Two-by-four mesh gives excellent results, but six-foot-high chain link fencing set in cement not only always looks clean and neat but also will last for the lifetime of the kennel. The wooden stockade fencing can be used outside the chainlink fencing if you desire complete privacy.

Secure and strong gate latches and locks should be provided, of course. Not only are some neighborhood children a threat, but it will guard against dognappers.

TATTOOING

Ninety per cent success has been reported on the return of stolen or lost dogs that have been tattooed. More and more this simple, painless, inexpensive method of positive identification for dogs is being reported all over the United States. Long popular in Canada, along with nose prints, the idea gained interest in this country when dognapping started to soar as unscrupulous people began stealing dogs for resale to research laboratories. Pet dogs that wander off and lost hunting dogs have always been a problem. The success of tattooing has been significant.

Tattooing can be done by the veterinarian for a minor fee. There are several dog "registries" that will record your dog's number and help you locate it should it be lost or stolen. The number of the dog's American Kennel Club registration is most often used on thoroughbred dogs, or the owner's Social Security number in the case of mixed breeds. The best place for the tattoo is the groin. Some prefer the inside of an ear, and the American Kennel Club has ruled that the judges officiating at the AKC dog shows not penalize the dog for the tattoo mark.

The tattoo mark serves not only to identify your dog should it be lost or stolen, but offers positive identification in large kennels where several litters of the same approximate age are on the premises. It is a safety measure against unscrupulous breeders "switching" puppies. Any age is a proper age to tattoo, but for safety's sake, the sooner the better.

The buzz of the needle might cause your dog to be apprehensive, but the pricking of the needle is virtually painless. The risk of infection is negligible when done properly, and the return of your beloved pet may be the reward for taking the time to insure positive identification for your dog. Your local Kennel Club will know of a dog registry in your area.

OUTDOOR HOUSEBREAKING

If you are particular about your dog's behavior in the house, where you expect him to be clean and respectful of the carpets and furniture, you should also want him to have proper manners outdoors. Just because the property belongs to you doesn't necessarily mean he should be allowed to empty himself any place he chooses. Before long the entire yard will be fouled and odorous and the dog will be completely irresponsible on other people's property as well. Dogs seldom recognize property lines.

If your dog does not have his own yard fenced in, he should be walked on leash before being allowed to run free and before being

The John N. Hatfields' Beau Cheval Old English Sheepdog. The Hatfields live in West Chester, Pennsylvania.

Mizzen, Old English Sheepdog owned by David H. Kogen, of Maplewood, New Jersey.

Old English Sheepdogs love water! Here an Old English takes time out for a drink from the lake. A few seconds later he was in for a bath!

Do not tie your Sheepdog to a chain or rope! The staked-out dog can become tangled in its own moorings, is defenceless against other animals, and can begin to have temperament problems! You can see by the hang dog expression on the dog pictured above that the situation is intolerable.

Ch. Tamara's Belvadeare pulling a sled across the frozen lake at Tamara Kennels.

Beau Cheval's Great White Beard poses with a young friend, Miss Carter, in Ohio. The Beard was bred by M. J. Anderson, Beau Cheval Farms, Wycombe, Pennsylvania.

penned up in his own yard. He will appreciate his own run being kept clean. You will find that if he has learned his manners outside, his manners inside will be better. Good manners in "toilet training" are especially important with big dogs!

OTHER IMPORTANT OUTDOOR MANNERS

Excessive barking is perhaps the most objectionable habit a dog indulges in out of doors. It annoys neighbors and makes for a noisy dog in the house as well. A sharp jerk on the leash will stop a dog from excessive barking while walking; trees and shrubs around a dog run will cut down on barking if a dog is in his own run. However, it is unfair to block off his view entirely. Give him some view—preferably of his own home—to keep his interest. Needless to say, do not leave a dog that barks excessively out all night.

You will want your dog to bark at strangers, so allow him this privilege. Then after a few "alerting" barks tell the dog to be quiet (with the same word command each time). If he doesn't get the idea, put him on leash and let him greet callers with you at the door until he does get the idea.

Do not let your dog jump on visitors either. Leash training may be necessary to break this habit as well. As the dog jumps in the

Chewing a few bones in the backyard. Two of Steven Clofine's Old English Sheepdogs. Many a Bobtail has been reared on his farm.

air, pull back on the lead so that the dog is returned to the floor abruptly. If he attempts to jump up on you, carefully raise your knee and push him away by leaning against his chest.

Do not let your dog roam free in the neighborhood no matter how well he knows his way home. Especially do not let your dog roam free to empty himself on the neighbor's property or gardens!

A positive invitation to danger is to allow your dog to chase cars or bicycles. Throwing tin cans or chains out of car windows at them has been suggested as a cure, but can also be dangerous if they hit the dog instead of the street. Streams of water from a

Susan Smith and Tamara's Calla Lilly taking Best In Show at Chagrin Valley Kennel Club's Junior Handling competition in 1970. Calla was just nine months old then, but she is now pointed and is on her way to her championship. Owned by Tamara Kennels of Tammy and Marvin Smith in Brighton, Michigan.

"What was that?" Lady Penelope of Infield Hut hears a noise and wonders who approaches. Lady was one of the first Bobtails owned by Steven Clofine of Bernville, Pennsylvania.

garden hose or water pistol are the least dangerous, but leash control is still the most scientific and most effective.

If neighbors report that your dog barks or howls or runs from window to window while you are away, crate training or room training for short periods of time may be indicated. If you expect to be away for longer periods of time, put the dog in the basement or a single room where he can do the least damage. The best solution of all is to buy him another dog or cat for companionship. Let them enjoy each other while you are away and have them both welcome you home!

ROD McKUEN

This enchanting photograph of poet and singer Rod McKuen graced the cover of the 1973 Calendar and Datebook put together by the popular star who adores his four Old English Sheepdogs. The calendar was published by Cheval Books and distributed in the U.S. and Canada by Simon and Schuster: it features other photographs of the McKuen Bobtails throughout the pages of the calendar.

A dog and his horse. . . . The John N. Hatfields' Old English Sheepdog in the corral at the Hatfield home in West Chester, Pennsylvania.

DOG INSURANCE

Much has been said for and against canine insurance, and much more will be said before this kind of protection for a dog becomes universal and/or practical. There has been talk of establishing a Blue Cross-type plan similar to that now existing for humans. However, the best insurance for your dog is You! Nothing compensates for tender, loving care. Like the insurance policies for humans, there will be a lot of fine print in the contracts revealing that the dog is not covered after all. These limited conditions usually make the acquisition of dog insurance expensive and virtually worthless.

Blanket coverage policies for kennels or establishments which board or groom dogs can be an advantage, especially in transporting dogs to and from their premises. For the one dog owner, however,

Off and running! Satchit and Mizzen trying to catch Shanti. Three Bobtails owned by Steven Clofine, Divine Light Farms, Bernville, Pennsylvania.

Two young Rivermist Old English Sheepdogs photographed on a fall afternoon.

Another Best Of Breed win for Ch. Rags Shags Chaucer, with handler Dick Baum. Owner Gail Fletcher of Tucson, Arizona. Photo by Henry.

whose dog is a constant companion, the cost for limited coverage is not necessary.

THE HIGH COST OF BURIAL

Pet cemeteries are mushrooming across the nation. Here, as with humans, the sky can be the limit for those who wish to bury their pets ceremoniously. The costs of satin-lined caskets, grave stones, flowers, etc. run the gamut of prices to match the emotions and means of the owner. This is strictly a matter of what the bereaved owner wishes to do.

IN THE EVENT OF YOUR DEATH . . .

This is a morbid thought perhaps, but ask yourself the question, "If death were to strike at this moment, what would become of my beloved dogs?"

Perhaps you are fortunate enough to have a relative, friend or spouse who could take over immediately, if only on a temporary basis.

Which way did she go? An Old English waits patiently while his mistress shops . . . .

Provide definite instructions before a disaster occurs and your dogs are carted off to the pound, or stolen by commercially minded neighbors with "resale" in mind. It is a simple thing to instruct your lawyer about your wishes in the event of sickness or death. Leave instructions as to feeding, etc., posted on your kennel room or kitchen bulletin board, or wherever your kennel records are kept. Also, tell several people what you are doing and why. If you prefer to keep such instructions private, merely place them in sealed envelopes in a known place with directions that they are to be opened only in the event of your demise. Eliminate the danger of your animals suffering in the event of an emergency that prevents your personal care of them.

KEEPING RECORDS

Whether or not you have one dog, or a kennel full of them, it is wise to keep written records. It takes only a few moments to record dates of inoculations, trips to the vet, tests for worms, etc. It can avoid confusion or mistakes, or having your dog not covered with immunization if too much time elapses between shots because you have to guess at the last shot.

Make the effort to keep all dates in writing rather than trying to commit them to memory. A rabies injection date can be a problem if you have to recall that "Fido had the shot the day Aunt Mary got back from her trip abroad, and, let's see, I guess that was around the end of June."

In an emergency, these records may prove their value if your veterinarian cannot be reached and you have to use another, or if you move and have no case history on your dog for the new veterinarian. In emergencies, you do not always think clearly or accurately, and if dates, and types of serums used, etc., are a matter of record, the veterinarian can act more quickly and with more confidence.

An Old English Sheepdog and a St. Bernard, owned by Juan Gonzalez of Michigan, prove that large dogs can get along well together. Both dogs bred by Beau Cheval Farms, Wycombe, Pennsylvania.

CHAPTER 13

NUTRITION

FEEDING THE ADULT DOG

The puppies' schedule of four meals a day should drop to three and then to two, so that by the time the dog reaches one year of age, it is eating one meal a day.

Living bookends! . . .Old English Sheepdogs of Beau Cheval Farms pretend to be bookends especially for this photo. Owned and bred by Marlene Anderson of Wycombe, Pennsylvania.

The time when you feed him each day can be a matter of the dog's preference or your convenience, so long as once in every 24 hours the dog receives a meal that provides him with a complete, balanced diet. In addition, of course, fresh clean water should be available at all times.

There are many brands of dry food, kibbles and biscuits on the market which are all of good quality. There are also many varieties of canned dog food which are of good quality and provide a balanced diet for your dog. But, for those breeders and exhibitors who show their dogs, additional care is given to providing a few "extras" which enhance the good health and good appearance of show dogs.

A good meal or kibble mixed with water or beef broth and raw meat is perhaps the best ration to provide. In cold weather many breeders add suet or corn oil (or even olive or cooking oil) to the

American and Canadian Ch. Droverdale Yogi Bear. Yogi is a brother of the famous Ch. Droverdale Image of Polo, owned by the Bakers of Oxon Hill, Maryland.

Ch. Droverdale Tattered Patches, owned by Pat and Sandi Baker of Oxon Hill, Maryland. Patches will soon become an R.O.M. dam.

mixture and others make use of the bacon fat after breakfast by pouring it over the food.

Salting a dog's food in the summer helps replace the salt he "pants away" in the heat. Many breeders sprinkle the food with garlic powder to sweeten the dog's breath and prevent gas, especially in breeds that gulp or wolf their food and swallow a lot of air. We prefer garlic powder, the salt is too weak and the clove is too strong.

There are those, of course, who cook very elaborately for their dogs, which is not necessary if a good meal and meat mixture is provided. Many prefer to add vegetables, rice, tomatoes, etc., in with everything else they feed. As long as the extras do not throw the nutritional balance off, there is little harm, but no one thing should be fed to excess. Occasionally liver is given, as a treat at home. Fish, which most veterinarians no longer recommend even for cats, is fed to puppies, but should not be given in excess of once a week. Always remember: No one thing should be given as a total diet. Balance is most important; steak or 100 per cent meat can kill a dog.

In March of 1971, the National Research Council investigated a great stir in the dog fancy about the all-meat dog-feeding controversy. It was established that meat and meat by-products constitute a complete balanced diet for dogs only when it is further fortified with vitamins and minerals.

Therefore, a good dog chow or meal mixed with meat provides the perfect combination for a dog's diet. While the dry food is a complete diet in itself, the fresh meat additionally satisfies the dog's anatomically and physiologically meat-oriented appetite. While dogs are actually carnivores, it must be remembered that when they were feeding themselves in the wilds they ate almost the entire animal they captured, including its stomach contents. This provided some of the vitamins and minerals we must now add to the diet.

The standards for diets which claim to be "complete and balanced" are set by the Subcommittee on Canine Nutrition of the National Research Council (NRC) of the National Academy of Sciences. This is the official agency for establishing the nutritional requirements of dog foods. Most all foods sold for dogs and cats meet these requirements and manufacturers are proud to say so on

Beau Cheval's Homer tries his hand at driving the Beau Cheval Express. Passenger is Dalerie Anderson, daughter of co-author Marlene Anderson, owner of the Beau Cheval Farms.

their labels, so look for this when you buy. Pet food labels must be approved by the Association of American Feed Control Officials, Pet Foods Committee. Both the Food and Drug Administration and the Federal Trade Commission of the AAFCO define the word "balanced" when referring to dog food as:

"Balanced is a term which may be applied to pet food having all known required nutrients in a proper amount and proportion based upon the recommendations of a recognized authority (The National Research Council is one) in the field of animal nutrition, for a given set of physiological animal requirements."

With this much care given to your dog's diet, there can be little reason for not having happy well-fed dogs in proper weight and proportions for the show ring.

OBESITY

As we mentioned above, there are many "perfect" diets for your dogs on the market today, that when fed in proper proportions should keep your dogs in "full bloom." However, there are those owners who, more often than not, indulge their own appetites and are inclined to overfeed their dogs as well. A study in Great Britain in the early 1970's found a major percentage of obese people also had obese dogs. The entire family was overfed and all suffered from the same condition.

Obesity in dogs is a direct result of the animal's being fed more food than he can properly "burn up" over a period of time, so it is stored as fat or fatty tissue in the body. Pet dogs are more inclined to become obese than show dogs or working dogs, but obesity also is a factor to be considered with the older dog since his exercise is curtailed.

A lack of "tuck up" on a dog, or not being able to feel the ribs, or great folds of fat which hang from the underside of the dog can all be considered as obesity. Genetic factors may enter into the picture, but usually the owner is at fault.

The life span of the obese dog is decreased on several counts. Excess weight puts undue stress on the heart as well as the joints. The dog becomes a poor anesthetic risk and has less resistance to viral or bacterial infections. Treatment is seldom easy or completely effective, so emphasis should be placed on not letting your dog get FAT in the first place!

CHAPTER 14

GERIATRICS

If you originally purchased good healthy stock and cared for your dog throughout his life, there is no reason why you cannot expect your dog to live to a ripe old age. With research and the remarkable foods specially produced for dogs this past decade or so, your dog's chances of longevity are increasing as each day goes by. If you have cared for him well your dog will be a sheer delight in his old age, just as he was while in his prime.

We can assume you have fed him properly (we hope he is not too fat! And have you ever noticed how fat people usually have fat dogs because they indulge their dogs' appetites as they do their own?) and that there has been no great illness; if so, you will find that very little additional care and attention need be given to keep him well. Exercise is still essential, as is the good food, booster shots, and tender loving care.

If a heart condition has developed there is still no reason to believe your dog cannot live to a good age. A diet, medication, and limited exercise might be all that is necessary to keep the condition under control. In the case of deafness or partial blindness, additional care must be taken to protect the dog, but the condition will in no way shorten his life. But prolonged exposure to temperature variations, over-eating, excessive exercise, lack of sleep or younger, more active dogs may take an unnecessary toll on the dog's energies and introduce serious trouble. Good judgment, periodic veterinary checkups, and individual attention will keep your dog with you for many added years.

When discussing geriatrics the question of at what age does a dog become old or aged usually is asked. The old saying is—and all it really is, actually, is pure conjecture—that every year of a dog's life is equal to seven years in a human. This theory is strictly a matter

A girl named Kim and a dog named Boo, and both belonging to Mrs. Marcia K. Violante of York, Pennsylvania.

A study of a windblown Beau Chevals Honey Fitz, owned by Bernadette A. Roeder of Mechanicsburg, Pennsylvania.

Muriel Skidell submits this charming photograph of a boy and his dog. . . . The dog's name is Biscuit, and it was bred by Beau Cheval Farms in Wycombe, Pennsylvania.

A lovely headstudy of a Bobtail belonging to Mr. and Mrs. John N. Hatfield of West Chester, Pennsylvania.

of opinion, and must remain so, since so many outside factors enter into how quickly each individual dog "ages." Recently a new chart has been devised which bears a more realistic equivalent in view of today's modern longevity records. The chart, which may help you determine a human age comparable for your dog, appears here.

DOG	MAN
6 months	10 years
1 year	15 years
2 years	24 years
3 years	28 years
4 years	32 years
5 years	36 years
6 years	40 years
7 years	44 years
8 years	48 years
9 years	52 years
10 years	56 years
15 years	76 years
21 years	100 years

It must be remembered that such things as serious illnesses, poor food and housing, general neglect and poor beginnings as puppies will all take their toll on a dog's general health and age him more quickly than a dog that has led a normal, healthy life. Let your veterinarian help you determine an age bracket for your dog in his later years.

While all your good care should prolong your dog's life, there are several "old age" disorders to be on the lookout for no matter how well he may be going. The tendency toward obesity is the most common, but constipation is another. Ageing teeth and slowing down of the digestive processes may hinder digestion and cause constipation, just as any major change in diet will bring on diarrhea in some instances. There is also the possibility of loss or impairment of hearing and eyesight which will also tend to make the dog wary and distrustful. Other behavioral changes may result as well, with crankiness, loss of patience, and lack of interest being the most obvious changes. But other ailments may manifest themselves in the form of rheumatism, arthritis, tumors and warts, heart disease, kidney infections and prostatitis in males, female disorders in

Charming frontal view of a typical Old English Sheepdog puppy sold by Beau Cheval Kennels to the family of Muriel Skidell. Biscuit was lost in a tragic accident recently.

Beau Chevals Short Notice, puppy bitch owned by Charles L. Marciante and M. J. Anderson. Sired by Beau Cheval's Ibsen and out of Beau Cheval's Bunny Rose, Short Notice was bred by Robert Yetter.

Beau Cheval's Winkin poses at five weeks of age. Bred by the Beau Cheval Kennels of Marlene Anderson, Wycombe, Pennsylvania.

bitches. And, of course, all of these require veterinary checking out as to degree of seriousness and proper treatment.

In all cases, avoid infectious diseases, because they debilitate older dogs to an alarming degree, also leaving them open to more serious complications and possibly death.

CHAPTER 15

YOUR DOG, YOUR VETERINARIAN AND YOU!

The purpose of this chapter is to explain why you should never attempt to be your own veterinarian. Quite the contrary, we urge emphatically that you establish good liaison with a reputable veterinarian who will help you maintain happy, healthy dogs. Our purpose is to bring you up to date on the discoveries made in modern canine medicine and to help you work with your veterinarian by applying these new developments to your own animals.

We have provided here "thumbnail" histories of many of the most common types of diseases your dog is apt to come in contact with during his lifetime. We feel that if you know a little something about the diseases and how to recognize their symptoms, your chances of catching them in the preliminary stages will help you and your veterinarian effect a cure before a serious condition develops.

Today's dog owner is a realistic, intelligent person who learns more and more about his dog—inside and out—so that he can care for and enjoy the animal to the fullest. He uses technical terms for parts of the anatomy, has a fleeting knowledge of the miracles of surgery and is fully prepared to administer clinical care for his animals at home. This chapter is designed for study and/or reference and we hope you will use it to full advantage.

We repeat, we do *not* advocate your playing "doctor." This includes administering medication without veterinary supervision, or even doing your own inoculations. General knowledge of diseases, their symptoms and side effects will assist you in diagnosing diseases for your veterinarian. He does not expect you to be an expert, but will appreciate your efforts in getting a sick dog to him before it is too late and he cannot save its life.

Patches, waiting for the children to come home on the school bus! Patches is owned by Warren Segal of Philadelphia.

ASPIRIN: NO PANACEA

There is a common joke about doctors telling their patients, when they telephone with a complaint, to take an aspirin, go to bed and let him know how things are in the morning! Unfortunately, that is exactly the way it turns out with a lot of dog owners who think aspirins are curealls and give them to their dogs indiscriminately. Then they call the veterinarian when the dog has an unfavorable reaction.

Aspirins are not panaceas for everything—certainly not for every dog. In an experiment, fatalities in cats treated with aspirin in one laboratory alone numbered ten out of 13 within a two-week period. Dogs' tolerance was somewhat better, as far as actual fatalities, but there was considerable evidence of ulceration in varying degrees on the stomach linings when necropsy was performed.

. Aspirin has been held in the past to be almost as effective for dogs as for people when given for many of the everyday aches and pains. The fact remains, however, that medication of any kind should be administered only after veterinary consultation and a specific dosage suitable to the condition is recommended.

While aspirin is chiefly effective in reducing fever, relieving minor pains and cutting down on inflammation, the acid has been proven harmful to the stomach when given in strong doses. Only your veterinarian is qualified to determine what that dosage is, or whether it should be administered to your particular dog at all.

WHAT THE THERMOMETER CAN TELL YOU

You will notice in reading this chapter dealing with the diseases of dogs that practically everything a dog might contract in the way of sickness has basically the same set of symptoms. Loss of appetite, diarrhea, dull eyes, dull coat, warm and/or runny nose, and FEVER!

Therefore, it is most advisable to have a thermometer on hand for checking temperature. There are several inexpensive metal rectal-type thermometers that are accurate and safer than the glass variety which can be broken. This may happen either by dropping, or perhaps even breaking off in the dog because of improper insertion or an aggravated condition with the dog that makes him violently resist the injection of the thermometer. Either kind should be lubricated with vaseline to make the insertion as easy as possible, after it has been sterilized with alcohol.

The normal temperature for a dog is 101.5° Farenheit, as compared to the human 98.6°. Excitement, as well as illness can cause this to vary a degree or two, but any sudden or extensive rise in body temperature must be considered as cause for alarm. Your first indication will be that your dog feels unduly "warm" and this is the time to take the temperature, not when the dog becomes very ill or manifests additional serious symptoms. With a thermometer on hand, you can check temperatures quickly and perhaps prevent some illness from becoming serious.

COPROPHAGY

Perhaps the most unpleasant of all phases of dog breeding is to come up with a dog that takes to eating stool. This practice, which is referred to politely as coprophagy, is one of the unsolved mysteries in the dog world. There simply is no explanation to why some dogs do it.

However, there are several logical theories, all or any of which may be the cause. Some say nutritional deficiencies; another says that dogs inclined to gulp their food (which passes through them not entirely digested) find it still partially palatable. There is another theory that the preservatives used in some meat are responsible for an appealing odor that remains through the digestive process. Then again poor quality meat can be so tough and unchewable, the dog swallows it whole and it passes through them in large undigested chunks.

There are others who believe the habit is strictly psychological, the result of a nervous condition or insecurity. Others believe the dog cleans up after itself, because it is afraid of being punished as it was when it made a mistake on the carpet as a puppy. Others claim boredom is the reason, or even spite. Others will tell you a dog does not want its personal odor on the premises for fear of attracting other hostile animals to itself or its home.

The most logical of all explanations and the one most veterinarians are inclined to accept is that it is a deficiency of dietary enzymes. Too much dry food can be bad and many veterinarians suggest trying meat tenderizers, monosodium glutamate, or garlic powder which gives the stool a bad odor and discourages the dog. Yeast or certain vitamins, or a complete change of diet are even more often suggested. By the time you try each of the above you will probably discover that the dog has outgrown the habit anyway. However, the condition cannot be ignored if you are to enjoy your dog to the fullest.

There is no set length of time that the problem persists, and the only real cure is to walk the dog on leash, morning and night and after every meal. In other words, set up a definite eating and exercising schedule before coprophagy is an established pattern.

Ch. Bobtail Keri of Droverdale, owned by Pat and Sandi Baker of Oxon Hill, Maryland. Keri will be campaigned as a special bitch by the Bakers.

Another lovely Droverdale R.O.M. dam, Ch. Droverdale BB Derry Aire, owned by Pat and Sandi Baker of Oxon Hill, Maryland. Photo by Graham.

Visiting day! A Poodle comes to call on Lance at the home of the Edward Beegles in Holicong, Pennsylvania.

MASTURBATION

A source of embarrassment to many dog owners, masturbation can be eliminated with a minimum of training.

The dog which is constantly breeding anything and everything, including the leg of the piano or perhaps the leg of your favorite guest, can be broken of the habit by stopping its cause.

The over-sexed dog—if truly that is what he is—which will never be used for breeding can be castrated. The kennel stud dog can be broken of the habit by removing any furniture from his quarters or keeping him on leash and on verbal command when he is around people, or in the house where he might be tempted to breed pillows, people, etc.

Hormone imbalance may be another cause and your veterinarian may advise injections. Exercise can be of tremendous help. Keeping the dog's mind occupied by physical play when he is around people will also help relieve the situation.

Females might indulge in sexual abnormalities like masturbation during their heat cycle, or again, because of a hormone imbalance. But if they behave this way because of a more serious problem, a hysterectomy may be indicated.

A sharp "no!" command when you can anticipate the act, or

a sharp "no!" when caught in the act will deter most dogs if you are consistent in your correction. Hitting or other physical abuse will only confuse a dog.

RABIES

The greatest fear in the dog fancy today is still the great fear it has always been—rabies!

What has always held true about this dreadful disease still holds true today. The only way rabies can be contracted is through the saliva of a rabid dog entering the bloodstream of another animal or person. There is, of course, the Pasteur treatment for rabies which is very effective. There was of late the incident of a little boy bitten by a rabid bat having survived the disease. However, the Pasteur treatment is administered immediately, if there is any question of

St. Bernard Beau Chevals Jake and his Old English Sheepdog friend, Yum Yum, take a rest in the cool grass . . . friendly breeds though they come from different countries.

exposure. Even more than dogs being found to be rabid, we now know that the biggest carriers are bats, skunks, foxes, rabbits and other warm-blooded animals, which pass it from one to another, since they do not have the benefit of inoculation. Dogs that run free should be inoculated for protection against these animals. For city or house dogs that never leave their owner's side, it may not be as necessary.

For many years, Great Britain, because it is an island and because of the country's strictly enforced six-month quarantine, was entirely free of rabies. But in 1969, a British officer brought back his dog from foreign duty and the dog was found to have the disease soon after being released from quarantine. There was a great uproar about it, with Britain killing off wild and domestic animals in a great scare campaign, but the quarantine is once again down to six months and things seem to have returned to a normal, sensible attitude.

Health departments in rural towns usually provide rabies inoculations free of charge. If your dog is outdoors a great deal, or exposed to other animals that are, you might wish to call the town hall and get information on the program in your area. One cannot be too cautious about this dread disease. While the number of cases diminishes each year, there are still thousands being reported and there is still the constant threat of an outbreak where animals roam free. And never forget, there is no cure.

Rabies is caused by a neurotropic virus which can be found in the saliva, brain and sometimes the blood of the warm-blooded animal afflicted. The incubation period is usually two weeks or as long as six months, which means you can be exposed to it without any visible symptoms. As we have said, while there is still no known cure, it can be controlled. It is up to every individual to help effect this control by reporting animal bites, educating the public to the dangers and symptoms and prevention of it, so that we may reduce the fatalities.

There are two kinds of rabies, one form is called "furious," and the other is referred to as "dumb." The mad dog goes through several stages of the disease. His disposition and behavior change radically and suddenly; he becomes irritable and vicious; the eating habits alter, and he rejects food for things like stones and sticks; he becomes exhausted and drools saliva out of his mouth almost

Champion Rivermist Blue Sage, photographed by photographer Joan Ludwig while taking a recent win.

constantly. He may hide in corners, look glassy eyed and suspicious, bite at the air as he races around snarling and attacking with his tongue hanging out. At this point paralysis sets in, starting at the throat so that he can no longer drink water though he desires it desperately; hence, the term hydrophobia is given. He begins to stagger and eventually convulse and death is imminent.

In "dumb" rabies paralysis is swift, the dog seeks dark, sheltered places and is abnormally quiet. Paralysis starts with the jaws, spreads down the body and death is quick. Contact by humans or other animals with the drool from either of these types of rabies on open skin can produce the fatal disease, so extreme haste and proper diagnosis is essential. In other words, you do not have to be bitten by a rabid dog to have the virus enter your system. An open wound or cut that comes in touch with the saliva is all that is needed.

Tops in the breed again! Left, Ch. Bobtail Acres Sno-Cone, the top-winning bitch in the midwest in 1970; on the right, Ch. Droverdale Image of Polo. Both Old English owned and shown by Pat and Sandi Baker of Oxon Hill, Maryland.

Ch. Bear Creek Ocita, better known as Bonnie, owned by Agnes and Patricia Miller, owners of the Blandford Kennels in Imlay City, Michigan.

The incubation and degree of infection can vary. You usually contract the disease faster if the wound is near the head, since the virus travels to the brain through the spinal cord. The deeper the wound, the more saliva is injected into the body, the more serious the infection. So, if bitten by a dog under any circumstances—or any warm-blooded animal for that matter—immediately wash out the wound with soap and water, bleed it profusely, and see your doctor as soon as possible.

Also, be sure to keep track of the animal that bit, if at all possible. When rabies is suspected the public health officer will need to send the animal's head away to be analyzed. If it is found to be rabies free, you will not need to undergo treatment. Otherwise, your doctor may advise that you have the Pasteur treatment, which is extremely painful. It is rather simple, however, to have the veterinarian examine a dog for rabies without having the dog sent away for positive diagnosis of the disease. A ten-day quarantine is usually all that is necessary for everyone's peace of mind.

Rabies is no respecter of age, sex or geographical location. It is found all over the world from North pole to South pole, and has nothing to do with the old wives' tale of dogs going mad in the hot summer months. True, there is an increase in reported cases during summer, but only because that is the time of the year for animals to roam free in good weather and during the mating season when the battle of the sexes is taking place. Inoculation and a keen eye for symptoms and bites on our dogs and other pets will help control the disease until the cure is found.

VACCINATIONS

If you are to raise a puppy, or a litter of puppies, successfully, you must adhere to a realistic and strict schedule of vaccination. Many puppyhood diseases can be fatal—all of them are debilitating. According to the latest statistics, 98 per cent of all puppies are being inoculated after 12 weeks of age against the dread distemper, hepatitis, and leptospirosis and manage to escape these horrible infections. Orphaned puppies should be vaccinated every two weeks until the age of 12 weeks. Distemper and hepatitis live-virus vaccine should be used, since they are not protected with the colostrum normally supplied to them through the mother's milk. Puppies weaned at six to seven weeks should also be inoculated repeatedly because they will no longer be receiving mother's milk. While not all will receive protection from the serum at this early age, it should be given and they should be vaccinated once again at both nine and 12 weeks of age.

Leptospirosis vaccination should be given at four months of age with thought given to booster shots if the disease is known in the area, or in the case of show dogs which are exposed on a regular basis to many dogs from far and wide. While annual boosters are in order for distemper and hepatitis, every two or three years is sufficient for leptospirosis, unless there is an outbreak in your immediate area. The one exception should be the pregnant bitch since there is reason to believe that inoculation might cause damage to the fetus.

Strict observance of such a vaccination schedule will not only keep your dog free of these debilitating diseases, but will prevent an

Gin-Gin, the Old English Sheepdog owned by Lorraine D'Essen, takes to the keyboard. Gin-Gin has been used in many commercial advertisements . . . a real "working" dog, so to speak!

epidemic in your kennel, or in your locality, or to the dogs which are competing at the shows.

GASTRIC TORSION

Gastric torsion or bloat, sometimes referred to more simply in the fancy as "twisted stomach," has become more and more prevalent. Dogs that in the past had been thought to die of blockage of the stomach or intestines because they had swallowed toys or rubber balls or other foreign objects are now known to have very probably been the victims of gastric torsion and the bloat that followed.

Though life can be saved by immediate surgery to untwist the organ, the rate of fatality is high. Symptoms of gastric torsion are unusual restlessness, excessive salivation, attempts to vomit, rapid respiration, pain and the eventual bloating of the abdominal region.

The cause of gastric torsion can be attributed to overeating, excess gas formation in the stomach, poor function of the stomach or intestine, blockage to entrances or exits to the stomach or intestine, or general lack of exercise. As the food ferments in the stomach, gases form which may twist the stomach in a clockwise direction, when the gas is unable to escape. Surgery where actually the stomach is untwisted counter-clockwise is the safest and most successful way to correct the situation.

The condition itself has no limit to size or breed of dog, so to avoid the threat of gastric torsion it is wise to keep your dog well exercised to be sure the body is functioning normally, make sure that food and water are available for the dog at all times, thereby reducing the tendency to overeat. Self service feeding, where the dog is able to eat off and on during the day, is recommended since there is not the urge to "stuff" at one time.

If you notice any of the symptoms of gastric torsion, call your veterinarian *immediately!*

SNAKEBITE

As field trials and hunts and the like become more and more popular with dog enthusiasts, the incident of snakebite becomes more of a likelihood. Dogs that are kept outdoors in runs or dogs that work the fields and roam on large estates are also likely victims.

Most veterinarians carry snakebite serum, and snakebite kits are sold to dog owners for just such purpose. To catch a snakebite in time might mean the difference between life and death, and whether your area is populated with snakes or not, it behooves you to know what to do in case it happens to you or your dog.

Your primary concern should be to get to a doctor or veterinarian immediately. The victim should be kept as quiet as possible (excitement or activity spreads the venom through the body more quickly) and if possible the wound should be bled enough to clean it out before applying a tourniquet, if the bite is severe.

First of all, it must be determined if the bite is from a poisonous or non-poisonous snake. If the bite carries two horseshoe shaped pinpoints of a double row of teeth, the bite can be assumed to be non-poisonous. If the bite leaves two punctures or holes—the result of the two fangs carrying venom—the bite is very definitely poisonous and time is of the essence.

Recently, physicians have come up with an added help in the case of snakebite. A first aid treatment referred to as Hypothermia, which is the application of ice to the wound to lower body tempera-

Closeup of Patches, an Old English Sheepdog owned by Mr. Warren Segal of Philadelphia.

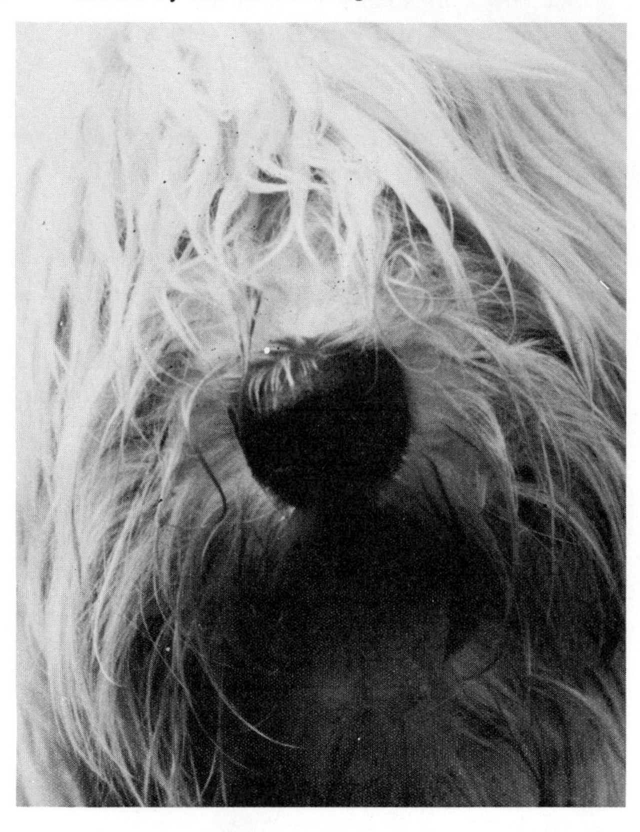

ture to a point where the venom spreads less quickly, minimizes swelling, helps prevent infection and has some influence on numbing the pain. If fresh water ice is not readily available, the bite may be soaked in ice cold water. But even more urgent is the need to get the victim to a hospital or a veterinarian for additional treatment.

EMERGENCIES

No matter how well you run your kennel or keep an eye on an individual dog, there will almost invariably be some emergency at some time that will require quick treatment until you get the animal to the veterinarian. The first and most important thing to remember is to keep calm! You will think more clearly and your animal will need to know he can depend on you to take care of him. However, he will be frightened and you must beware of fear biting. Therefore, do not shower him with kisses and endearments at this time, no matter how sympathetic you feel. Comfort him reassuringly, but keep your wits about you. Before getting him to the veterinarian try to alleviate the pain and shock.

If you can take even a minor step in this direction it will be a help toward the final cure. Listed here are a few of the emergencies which might occur and what you can do AFTER you have called the vet and told him you are coming.

Burns

If you have been so foolish as not to turn your pot handles toward the back of the stove—for your children's sake as well as your dog's—and the dog is burned, apply vaseline or butter and treat for shock. The covering will help prevent secondary infection if the burns are severe. Electrical or chemical burns are treated the same; but with an acid or alkali burn, use, respectively, a bicarbonate of soda or vinegar solution. Then apply vaseline. Check this with the veterinarian when you call him.

Drowning

Most animals love the water, but sometimes get in "over their heads." Should your dog take in too much water, hold him upside down and open his mouth so that water can empty from the lungs, then apply artificial respiration, or mouth-to-mouth resuscitation. Then treat for shock by covering him with a blanket, administering a stimulant such as coffee with sugar, and soothing him with voice and hand.

A marvelous picture of Dr. and Mrs. Hugh Jordan's Old English Sheepdogs waiting for a ride in their old London taxi. The Jordans own the Loyalblu Kennels, Reg, in Whittier, California.

Fits and Convulsions

Prevent the dog from thrashing about and injuring himself. cover with a blanket and hold down until you can get him to the veterinarian.

Frostbite

There is no excuse for an animal getting frostbite if you are on your toes and care for the animal. However, should frostbite set in, thaw out the affected area slowly with a circulatory motion and stimulation. Use vaseline to help keep the skin from peeling off and/or drying out.

Heart Attack

Be sure the animal keeps breathing by applying artificial respiration. A mild stimulant may be used and give him plenty of air. Treat for shock as well, and get to the veterinarian quickly.

Suffocation

Artificial respiration and treat for shock with plenty of air.

Sun Stroke

Cooling the dog off immediately is essential. Ice packs, submersion in ice water, and plenty of cool air are needed.

Wounds

Open wounds or cuts which produce bleeding must be treated with hydrogen peroxide and tourniquets should be used if bleeding is excessive. Also, shock treatment must be given and keep him warm.

THE FIRST AID KIT

It would be sheer folly to try to operate a kennel or to keep a dog without providing for certain emergencies that are bound to crop up when there are active dogs around. Just as you would provide a first aid kit for people you should also provide a first aid kit for the animals on the premises.

The first aid kit should contain the following items:

- BFI or other medicated powder
- jar of vaseline
- Q-tips
- bandage—1 inch gauze
- adhesive tape
- bandaids
- cotton
- boric acid powder

A trip to your veterinarian is always safest, but there are certain preliminaries for cuts and bruises of a minor nature that you can care for yourself.

Cuts, for instance, should be washed out and medicated powder or vaseline applied with a bandage. The lighter the bandage the better so that the most air possible can reach the wound. Q-tips can be used for removing debris from the eyes after which a mild

Ch. Tamara's Mighty Mimsy shown winning toward her championship, which was completed with four majors. Her sire was the great Ch. Tempest of Dalcroy, her dam, Ch. Tamara's Patches of Perse. Owned and bred by the Marvin Smiths, Tamara Kennels, Brighton, Michigan.

solution of boric acid wash can be applied. Burns can be assuaged by an application of vaseline. As for sores, use dry powder on wet sores, and vaseline on dry sores. Use cotton for washing out wounds and drying them.

A particular caution must be given here on bandaging. Make sure that the bandage is not too tight to hamper the dog's circulation.

Also, make sure the bandage is made correctly so that the dog does not bite at it trying to get it off. A great deal of damage can be done to a wound by a dog tearing at a bandage to get it off. If you notice the dog is starting to bite at it, do it over or put something on the bandage that smells and tastes bad to him. Make sure, however, that the solution does not soak through the bandage and enter the wound. Sometimes, if it is a leg wound, a sock or stocking slipped on the dog's leg will cover the bandage edges and will also keep it clean.

HOW NOT TO POISON YOUR DOG

Ever since the appearance of Rachel Carson's book *Silent Spring*, people have been asking, "Just how dangerous are chemicals?" In the animal world where disinfectants, room deodorants, parasitic sprays, solutions and aerosols are so widely used, the question has taken on even more meaning. Veterinarians are beginning to ask, "What kind of disinfectant do you use?" or "Have you any fruit trees that have been sprayed recently?" when animals are brought in to their offices in a toxic condition, or for unexplained death, or when entire litters of puppies die mysteriously, there is good reason to ask such questions.

The popular practice of protecting animals against parasites has given way to their being exposed to an alarming number of commercial products, some of which are dangerous to their very lives. Even flea collars can be dangerous, especially if they get wet or somehow touch the genital regions or eyes. While some products are a great deal more poisonous than others, great care must be taken that they be applied in proportion to the size of the dog and the area to be covered. Many a dog has been taken to the vet with an unusual skin problem that was a direct result of having been bathed with a detergent rather than a proper shampoo. Certain products that are safe for dogs can be fatal for cats. Extreme care must be taken to read all ingredients and instructions carefully before use on any animal.

The same caution must be given to outdoor chemicals. Dog owners must question the use of fertilizers on their lawns. Lime, for instance, can be harmful to a dog's feet. The unleashed dog that covers the neighborhood on his daily rounds is open to all sorts of tree and lawn sprays and insecticides that may prove harmful to

A win several years ago for Ch. King's Messenger at the Chagrin Valley Kennel Club in Gates Mills, Ohio. Dr. Thomas D. Buck was the judge, with M. H. Anderson presenting the trophy to handler and owner Stanley F. Kraft of Cleveland, Ohio. William Brown photograph.

him, if not as a poison, as a producer of an allergy. Many puppy fatalities are reported when they consume mothballs.

There are various products found around the house which can be lethal, such as rat poison, boric acid, hand soap, detergents, and insecticides. The garage too may provide dangers: Antifreeze for the car, lawn, garden and tree sprays, paints, etc., are all available for tipping over and consuming. All poisons should be placed on high shelves for the sake of your children as well as your animals.

Perhaps the most readily available of all household poisons are plants. Household plants are almost all poisonous, even if taken in small quantities. Some of the most dangerous are the Elephant Ear, the Narcissus bulb, any kind of ivy leaves, Burning Bush leaves, the Jimson weed, the Dumb Cane weed, mock orange fruit, Castor Beans, Scotch Broom seeds, the root or seed of the plant called Four O'Clock, Cyclamen, Pimpernel, Lily of the Valley, the stem of the Sweet Pea, Rhododendrons of any kind, Spider Lily bulbs, Bayonet root, Foxglove leaves, Tulip bulbs, Monkshood roots, Azalea, Wisteria, Poinsettia leaves, Mistletoe, Hemlock, Locoweed and Arrowglove. In all, there are over 500 poisonous plants in the United States. Peach, elderberry and cherry trees can cause cyanide poisoning if the bark is consumed. Rhubarb leaves either raw or cooked can cause death or violent convulsions. Check out your closets, fields and grounds around your home to see what might be of danger to your pets.

SYMPTOMS OF POISONING

Be on the lookout for vomiting, hard or labored breathing, whimpering, stomach cramps, and trembling as a prelude to the convulsions. Any delay in a visit to your veterinarian can mean death. Take along the bottle or package or a sample of the plant you suspect to be the cause to help the veterinarian determine the correct antidote.

The most common type of poisoning which accounts for nearly one-fourth of all animal victims is staphylococcic-infected food. Salmonella ranks third. These can be avoided by serving fresh food and not letting it lie around in hot weather.

There are also many insect poisonings caused by animals eating cockroaches, spiders, flys, butterflies, etc. Toads and some frogs give off a fluid which can make a dog foam at the mouth—and even kill him—if he bites just a little too hard!

Some misguided dog owners think it is "cute" to let their dogs enjoy a cocktail with them before dinner. There can be serious effects resulting from encouraging a dog to drink—sneezing fits, injuries as a result of intoxication, and heart stoppage are just a few. Whiskey for medicinal purposes, or beer for brood bitches should be administered only on the advice of your veterinarian.

There have been cases of severe damage and death when dogs

emptied ash trays and consumed cigarettes, resulting in nicotine poisoning. Leaving a dog alone all day in a house where there are cigarettes available on a coffee table is asking for trouble. Needless to say, the same applies to marijuana. The narcotic addict who takes his dog along with him on "a trip" does not deserve to have a dog. All the ghastly side effects are as possible for the dog as for the addict, and for a person to submit an animal to this indignity is indeed despicable. Don't think it doesn't happen. Ask the veterinarians that practice near some of your major hippie havens! Unfortunately, in all our major cities the practice is becoming more and more a problem for the veterinarian.

Be on the alert and remember that in the case of any type of poisoning, the best treatment is prevention.

THE CURSE OF ALLERGY

The heartbreak of a child being forced to give up a beloved pet because he is suddenly found to be allergic to it is a sad but true story. Many families claim to be unable to have dogs at all; others seem to be able only to enjoy them on a restricted basis. Many children know animals only through occasional visits to a friend's house or the zoo.

While modern veterinary science has produced some brilliant allergists, such as Dr. Edward Baker of New Jersey, the field is still working on a solution for those who suffer from exposure to their pets. There is no permanent cure as yet.

Over the last quarter of a century there have been many attempts at a permanent cure, but none has proven successful, because the treatment was needed too frequently, or was too expensive to maintain over extended periods of time.

However, we find that most people who are allergic to their animals are also allergic to a variety of other things as well. By eliminating the other irritants, and by taking medication given for the control of allergies in general, many are able to keep pets on a restricted basis. This may necessitate the dog's living outside the house, being groomed at a professional grooming parlor instead of by the owner, or merely being kept out of the bedroom at night. A discussion of this "balance" factor with your medical and veterinary doctors may give new hope to those willing to try.

A paper presented by Mathilde M. Gould, M.D., a New York

Who says it takes four good legs to run like a dog? This Old English proves he can run, play, jump and be his charming self with one broken leg. Dog out of Beau Cheval's Bunny Rose and bred by Robert Yetter.

allergist, before the American Academy of Allergists in the 1960's, and reported in the September-October 1964 issue of the National Humane Review magazine, offered new hope to those who are allergic by a method referred to as hyposensitization. You may wish to write to the magazine and request the article for discussion with your medical and veterinary doctors on your individual problem.

DO ALL DOGS CHEW?

All young dogs chew! Chewing is the best possible method of cutting teeth and exercising gums. Every puppy goes through this teething process. True, it can be destructive if not watched carefully, and it is really the responsibility of every owner to prevent the damage before it occurs.

When you see a puppy pick up an object to chew, immediately remove it from his mouth with a sharp "No!" and replace the object with a toy or a rawhide bone which should be provided for him to do his serious chewing. Puppies take anything and everything into their mouths so they should be provided with proper toys which they cannot chew up and swallow.

Ch. Droverdale Image of Polo captured in a full action shot, when the dog was "moving out" in the show ring. Owners Pat and Sandi Baker of Oxon Hill, Maryland.

BONES

There are many opinions on the kind of bones a dog should have. Anyone who has lost a puppy or dog because of a bone chip puncturing the stomach or intestinal wall will say "no bones" except for the processed or rawhide kind you buy in pet shops. There are those who say shank or knuckle bones are permissible. Use your own judgment, but when there are adequate processed bones which you know to be safe, why risk a valuable animal? Cooked bones, soft enough to be pulverized and put in the food can be fed if they are reduced almost to a powder. If you have the patience for this sort of thing, okay. Otherwise, stick to the commercial products.

As for dogs and puppies chewing furniture, shoes, etc., replace the object with something allowable and safe and put yourself on record as remembering to close closet doors. Keep the puppy in the same room with you so you can stand guard over the furniture.

Electrical cords and sockets, or wires of any kind, present a dangerous threat to chewers. Glass dishes which can be broken are hazardous if not picked up right after feeding.

Chewing can also be a form of frustration or nervousness. Dogs sometimes chew for spite, if owners leave them alone too long or too often. Bitches will sometimes chew if their puppies are taken away from them too soon; insecure puppies often chew thinking they're nursing. Puppies which chew wool or blankets or carpet corners or certain types of materials may have a nutritional deficiency or something lacking in their diet, such as craving the starch that might be left in material after washing. Perhaps the articles have been near something that tastes good and they retain the odor.

The act of chewing has no connection with particular breeds or ages, any more than there is a logical reason for dogs to dig holes outdoors or dig on wooden floors indoors.

So we repeat, it is up to you to be on guard at all times until the need—or habit—passes.

HIP DYSPLASIA

Hip Dysplasia, or HD, is one of the most widely discussed of all animal afflictions, since it has appeared in varying degrees, in just about every breed of dog. True, the larger breeds seem most

Ch. Rivermist Blue Sage, pictured winning under judge Charles Hamilton for a five-point major at 10 months of age. Dick Baum handles for owner Gail Fletcher of Tucson, Arizona. Sage is sired by Ch. Unesta Pim ex Ch. Rivermist Hollyhock.

susceptible, but it has hit the small breeds and is beginning to be recognized in cats as well.

While HD in man has been recorded as far back as 370 B.C., HD in dogs was more than likely referred to as rheumatism until veterinary research came into the picture. In 1935, Dr. Otto Schales, at Angell Memorial Hospital in Boston, wrote a paper on

Lady Shanti of Infield Hut, a very fast bitch in the field and still a good house dog, owned by Steven Clofine, Bernville, Pennsylvania. Shanti is sired by Beau Chevals Sir Lancelot ex Lady Salina of Infield Hut.

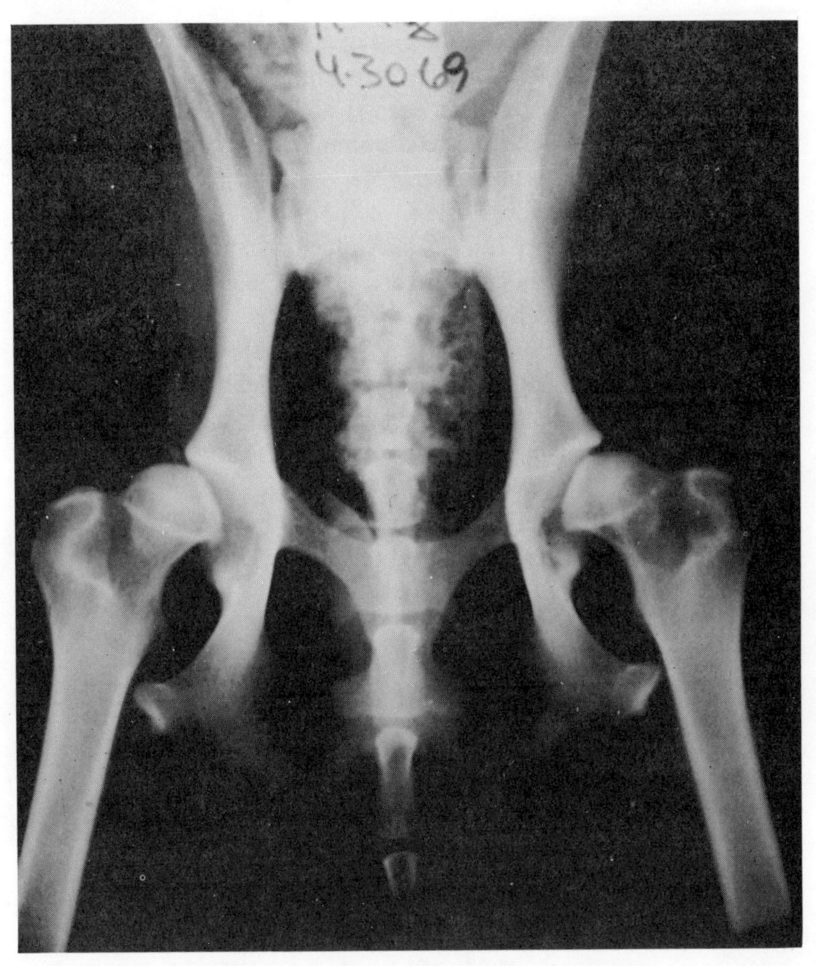

Dysplastic hips—incurable and hereditary.

Hip Dysplasia and classified the four degrees of dysplasia of the hip joint as follows:

Grade 1—slight (poor fit between ball and socket)

Grade 2—moderate (moderate but obvious shallowness of the socket)

Grade 3—severe (socket quite flat)

Grade 4—very severe (complete displacement of head of femur at early age)

HD is an incurable, hereditary, though not congenital disease of the hip sockets. It is transmitted as a dominant trait with irregular manifestations. Puppies appear normal at birth but the constant wearing away of the socket means the animal moves more and more on muscle, thereby presenting a lameness, a difficulty in getting up and severe pain in advanced cases.

The degree of severity can be determined around six months of age, but its presence can be noticed from two months of age. The problem is determined by X-ray, and if pain is present it can be relieved temporarily by medication. Exercise should be avoided since motion encourages the wearing away of the bone surfaces.

Dogs with HD should not be shown or bred, if quality in the breed is to be maintained. It is essential to check a pedigree for dogs known to be dysplastic before breeding, since this disease can be dormant for many generations. It has been estimated that 90 per cent of all Saints are affected to some degree.

ELBOW DYSPLASIA

The same condition can also affect the elbow joints and is known as Elbow Dysplasia. This also causes lameness, and dogs so affected should not be used for breeding.

PATELLAR DYSPLASIA

Some of the smaller breeds of dogs also suffer from Patella Dysplasia, or dislocation of the knee. This can be treated surgically, but the surgery by no means abolishes the hereditary factor. Therefore, these dogs should not be used for breeding.

All dogs—in any breed—should be X-rayed before being used for breeding. The X-ray should be read by a competent veterinarian, and the dog declared free and clear.

HD PROGRAM IN GREAT BRITAIN

The British Veterinary Association (BVA) has made an attempt to control the spread of HD by appointing a panel of members of their profession who have made a special study of the disease, to read X-rays. Dogs over one year of age may be X-rayed and certified as free. Forms are completed in triplicate to verify the tests. One copy remains with the panel, one copy is for the owner's veterinarian, and one for the owner. A record is also sent to the

British Kennel Club for those wishing to check on a particular dog for breeding purposes.

THE UNITED STATES REGISTRY

In the United States we have a central Hip Dysplasia Foundation, known as the OFA (Orthopedic Foundation for Animals). This HD control registry was formed in 1966. X-rays are sent for expert evaluation by qualified radiologists.

All you need do for complete information on getting an X-ray for your dog is to write to the Orthopedic Foundation for Animals

One of the four Best In Show wins for the great Droverdale Image of Polo. This win came under renowned judge Alva Rosenberg in November, 1970 and brought his total to 21 Group Firsts and 95 Bests of Breed, as well as two National Specialties. The Bakers, his proud owners, say they will retire Polo when he reaches an even 100 Bests of Breed. Photo by Martin Booth.

at 817 Virginia Ave., Columbia, Mo., 65201, and request their Dysplasia packet. There is no charge for this kit. It contains an envelope large enough to hold your X-ray film (which you will have taken by your own veterinarian), and a drawing showing how to position the dog properly for X-ray. There is also an application card for proper identification of the dog. Then, hopefully, your dog will be certified "normal." You will be given a registry number which you can put on his pedigree, use in your advertising, and rest assured your breeding program is in good order.

All X-rays should be sent to the address above. Any other information you might wish to have may be requested from Mrs. Robert Bower, OFA, Route 1, Constantine, Mo., 49042.

We cannot urge strongly enough the importance of doing this. While it involves time and effort, the reward in the long run will more than pay for your trouble. To see the heartbreak of parents and children when their beloved dog has to be put to sleep because of severe Hip Dysplasia as the result of bad breeding is a sad experience. Don't let this happen to you or to those who will purchase your puppies!

Additionally, we should mention that there is a method of palpation to determine the extent of affliction. This can be painful if the animal is not properly prepared for the examination. There have also been attempts to replace the animal's femur and socket. This is not only expensive, but the percentage of success is small.

For those who refuse to put their dog down, there is a new surgical technique which can relieve pain, but in no way constitutes a cure. This technique involves the severing of the pectinius muscle which, for some unknown reason brings relief from pain over a period of many months—even up to two years. Two veterinary colleges in the United States are performing this operation at the present time. However, the owner must also give permission to "de-sex" the dogs at the time of the muscle severance. This is a safety measure to help stamp out Hip Dysplasia, since obviously the condition itself remains and can be passed on.

HOT SPOTS

Many Old English will itch and scratch and almost overnight break out with a "hot spot" often mistakenly diagnosed as wet

Ch. Tempest of Dalcroy, sire of 21 champions to date and third top sire in the breed. Owned by the Marvin Smiths, Tamara Kennels, Brighton, Michigan.

eczema, dry eczema, mange, or perhaps something even worse! A hot spot is a place where the skin is raw, red and oozing with blood or pus. Veterinarians will sometimes prescribe cortisone, but cortisone can produce other problems and must be given with extreme caution. There is a simple "home remedy" which is very inexpensive and most convenient, and almost always works:

Take one fourth cup of laundry bleach to one full cup of water, and pour it over the affected area twice daily. Dust with corn starch in between times. If the area is raw and bloody, try to dry it up with corn starch first . . . but the bleach is necessary to effect a cure. Another treatment used by some of the old time breeders is tincture of green soap which can be purchased in any drug store. Others have achieved results with B.F.I. powder, or antibiotic wound powders or dressing powders also available at drug stores.

Diligent care is required to halt soreness and, of course, never shave the area. The dog can be ready for the show ring once again in a matter of days if treatment is begun before there is too great a loss of hair.

CHAPTER 16

THE BLIGHT OF PARASITES

Dogs can be afflicted by both internal and external parasites. The external parasites are known as fleas, ticks and lice. All of these, while bothersome, can be treated with sprays and bath dips and a lot of fortitude. However, the internal parasites, or worms of various kinds, are usually well-infested before discovery and require more substantial means of ridding the dog of them completely.

The most common of all is the round worm. This, like many other parasitic worms, is excreted in egg or larvae form and passed on to other dogs in this manner.

Worm medicine should be prescribed by a veterinarian, and dogs should be checked for worms at least twice a year, or every three months if there is a known epidemic in your area, and during the summer months when fleas (tapeworm carriers) are plentiful.

Other types of worms are hookworms, whipworms, tapeworms, heartworms, kidney and lung worms. Each can be peculiar to a part of the country or may be carried by a dog from one area to another. Symptoms for worms might be vomiting intermittently, eating grass, lack of pep, bloated stomach, rubbing tail along the ground, loss of weight, dull coat, anemia and pale gums, eye discharge, or unexplained nervousness and irritability.

Never worm a sick dog, or a pregnant bitch after the first two weeks, or a constipated dog which will retain the strong medicine within his body for too long a time. The best, safest way to determine the presence of worms is to test for them before they do excessive damage.

HOW TO TEST YOUR DOG FOR WORMS

Worms can kill your dog if the infestation is severe enough. Even light infestations of worms can debilitate a dog to the point where he is more susceptible to other serious diseases that can kill, if the worms do not.

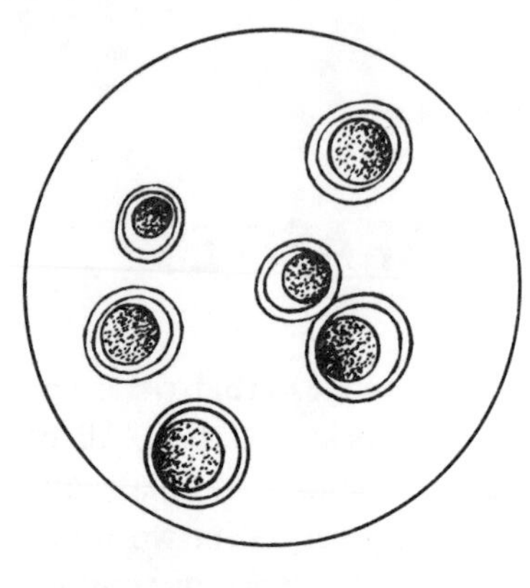

Round Worm
(Ascarid)

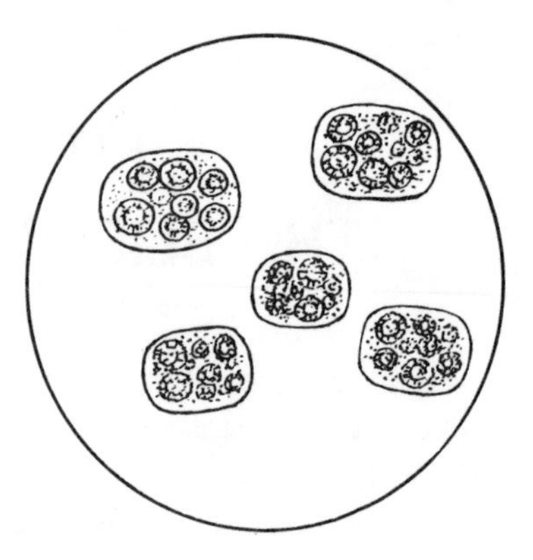

Tapeworm

Hookworm

Whipworm

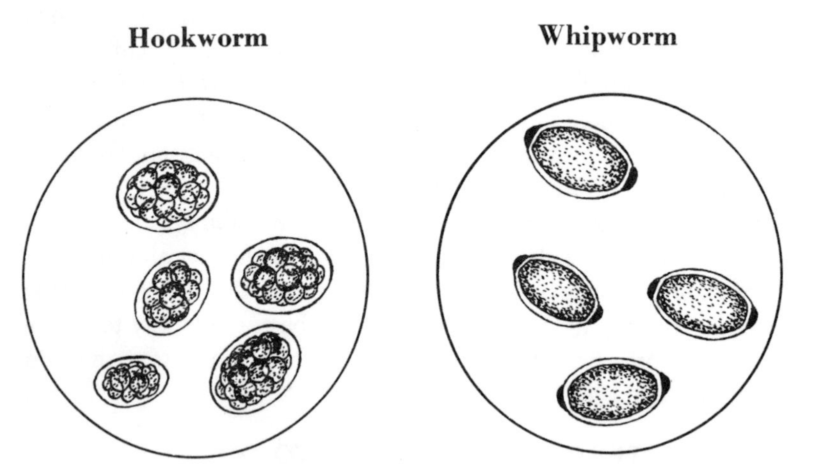

Eggs of certain parasites commonly seen in dogs.

An Old English Sheepdog Club of America Specialty in the 1950's with judge Mervin Rosenbaum officiating found his choice for Best of Breed to be Ch. December Snow, handled by Charles Meyer and owned by W. T. Houston of Mercer, Pennsylvania. Best of Opposite Sex (pictured at right being handled by Ed Carver) was Barclay Acheson's Ch. Peggy Ann of Bashurat. Photograph by Evelyn M. Shafer.

Today's medication for worming is relatively safe and mild, and worming is no longer the traumatic experience for either dog or owner that it used to be. Great care must be given, however, to the proper administration of the drugs. Correct dosage is a "must" and clean quarters are essential to rid your kennel of these parasites. It is almost impossible to find an animal that is completely free of parasites, so we must consider worming as a necessary evil.

However mild today's medicines may be, it is inadvisable to worm a dog unnecessarily. There are simple tests to determine the presence of worms and this chapter is designed to help you make these tests yourself. Veterinarians charge a nominal fee for this service, if it is not part of their regular office visit examination. It is a simple matter to prepare fecal slides that you can read yourself on a periodic basis. Over the years it will save you much time and money, especially if you have more than one dog.

All that is needed by way of equipment is a microscope with 10X power. These can usually be purchased in the toy department in a department store. These microscopes come with the necessary glass slides, equipment and attachments.

After the dog has defecated, take an applicator stick, or a toothpick with a flat end, or even an old-fashioned wooden matchstick, and gouge off a piece of the stool about the size of a small pea. Have one of the glass slides ready with a large drop of water on it. Mix the two together until you have a cloudy film over a large area of the slide. This smear should be covered with another slide, or a cover slip—though I have obtained readings with just the one open slide. Place your slide under the microscope and prepare to focus in on it. To read the slide you will find that your eye should follow a certain pattern. Start at the top and read from left to right, then right back to the left side and then left over to the right once again until you have looked at every portion of the slide from the top left to the bottom right side, as illustrated here:

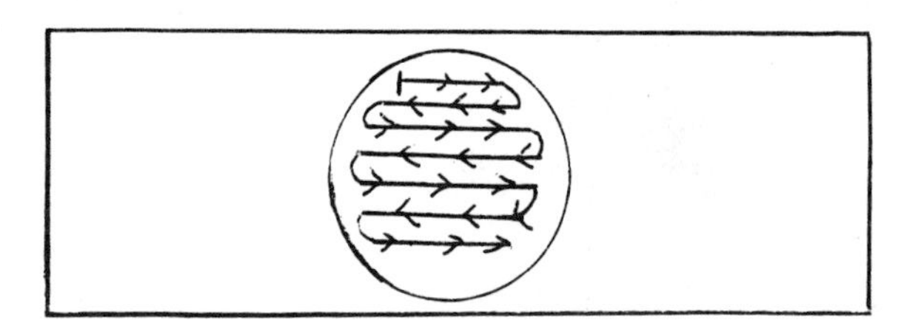

Make sure that your smear is not too thick or watery or the reading will be too dark and confused to make proper identification. If you would rather not make your own fecal examinations, but prefer to have the veterinarian do it, the proper way to present a segment of the stool for him to examine is as follows:

After the dog has defecated, a portion of the stool, say a square inch from different sections, should be placed in a glass jar and

Ch. Tara-Woods Blue Barron wins Group First at the Finger Lakes Kennel Club show in August, 1964, under judge Percy Roberts. Barron is owned by the Isaksons and is handled here by Howard Tyler. Photo by Stephen Klein.

labeled with the dog's name and the name and address of the owner. If the sample cannot be examined within three to four hours after passage, it should be refrigerated. Your opinion as to what variety of worms you suspect is sometimes helpful to the veterinarian and may be noted on the label of the jar you submit to him for examination.

Checking for worms is advisable not only for the welfare of the dog but for the protection of your family, since most worms are transmissible, under certain circumstances, to humans.

Jai Shri Satchitanand, Satchit (a word meaning truth, consciousness and bliss) for short. This lovely male is pictured at just 8 months of age. His dam is Lady Penelope of Infield Hut, his sire Beau Chevals Shango. Owned by Steven Clofine.

A photograph of a young Merriedip Master Pantaloons, future Best In Show winner, owned by Mrs. Lewis Roesler. This William Fox photograph was taken several years ago. Merriedip Master Pantaloons was a son of Ch. Dovenderry Volunteer and International Champion Mistress Petticoats of Pastorale.

CHAPTER 17

DICTIONARY OF DOG DISEASES

AN AID TO DIAGNOSIS

— A —

ABORTION—When a pregnancy is not right the embryos may be prematurely expelled from the uterus. Usually, the bitch makes a rapid recovery. Abortion can also be the result of an injury or accident which can cause complications. If part of a fetus is left in the uterus, serious infection may occur. The first indication of this will be high fever, dry nose and lethargy. The immediate services of a veterinarian are necessary.

ABSCESS—A skin eruption characterized by a localized collection of pus formed as a result of disintegrating tissues of the body. Abscesses may be acute or chronic. An acute abscess forms rapidly and will more than likely burst within a week. It is accompanied by pain, redness, heat and swelling, and may cause a rise in temperature. An abscess is usually the result of infection of a bacterial nature. Treatment consists of medication in the form of antibiotics and salves, ointments, powders or a poultice designed to bring it to a head. A chronic abscess is a slow-developing headless lump surrounded by gathering tissue. This infection is usually of internal origin, and painless unless found in a sensitive area of the body. The same antibiotics and medications are used. Because abscesses of this nature are slow in developing, they are generally slow in dissolving.

Ch. Silvershag Donnemary, the foundation bitch for Pat and Sandi Baker's Droverdale Kennels in Oxon Hill, Maryland. She is an R.O.M. dam of ten champions to date from just two litters . . . truly a remarkable achievement in the breed.

ACARUS—One of the parasitic mites which cause mange.

ACHONDROPLASIA—A disease which results in the stunting of growth, or dwarfing of the limbs before birth.

ADENOMA—A non-inflammatory growth or benign tumor found in a prominent gland; most commonly found in the mammary gland of the bitch.

AGALACTIA—A contagious, viral disease resulting in lowered or no production of milk by a nursing bitch. It usually occurs in warm weather, and is accompanied by fever and loss of appetite. Abscesses may also form. In chronic cases the mammary gland itself may atrophy.

ALARIASIS—An infection caused by flukes *(Alaria arisaemoides)*, which are ingested by the dog. They pass on to the bronchial tract and into the small intestine where they grow to maturity and feed on intestinal contents.

ALLERGY—Dogs can be allergic as well as people to outdoor or indoor surroundings, such as carpet fuzz, pillow stuffings, food, pollen, etc. Recent experiments in hyposensitization have proved effective in many cases when injections are given with follow-up "boosters." Sneezing, coughing, nasal discharges, runny, watery eyes, etc., are all symptomatic.

ALOPECIA—A bare spot, or lack of full growth of hair on a portion of the body; another name for baldness and can be the end result of a skin condition.

AMAUROSIS—Sometimes called "glass eye." A condition that may occur during a case of distemper if the nervous system has been affected, or head injuries sustained. It is characterized by the animal bumping into things or by a lack of coordination. The condition is incurable and sooner or later the optic nerve becomes completely paralyzed.

ANALGESIA—Loss of ability to feel pain with the loss of consciousness or the power to move a part of the body. The condition may be induced by drugs which act on the brain or central nervous system.

ANAL SAC OBSTRUCTION—The sacs on either side of the rectum, just inside the anus, at times may become clogged. If the condition persists, it is necessary for the animal to be assisted in their opening, so that they do not become infected and/or abscess. Pressure is applied by the veterinarian and the glands release a thick, horrible-smelling excretion. Antibiotics or a "flushing" of the glands if infected is the usual treatment, but at the first sign of discomfort in the dog's eliminating, or a "sliding along" the floor, it is wise to check for clogged anal glands.

ANASARCA—Dropsy of the connective tissues of the skin. It is occasionally encountered in fetuses and makes whelping difficult.

ANEMIA—A decrease of red blood cells which are the cells that carry oxygen to the body tissues. Causes are usually severe infestation of parasites, bad diet, or blood disease. Transfusions and medications can be given to replace red blood cells, but the disease is sometimes fatal.

ANEURYSM—A rupture or dilation of a major blood vessel, causing a bulge or swelling of the affected part. Blood gathers in the tissues forming a swelling. It may be caused by strain, injury, or when arteries are weakened by debilitating disease or old age. Surgery is needed to remove the clot.

ANESTROUS—When a female does not come into heat.

ANTIPERISTALSIS—A term given to the reverse action of the normal procedures of the stomach or intestine, which brings their contents closer to the mouth.

ANTIPYRETICS—Drugs or methods used to reduce temperature during fevers. These may take the form of cold baths, purgatives, etc.

ANTISPASMODICS—Medications which reduce spasms of the muscular tissues and soothe the nerves and muscles involved.

ANTISIALICS—Term applied to substances used to reduce excessive salivation.

ARSENIC POISONING—Dogs are particularly susceptible to this type of poisoning. There is nausea, vomiting, stomach pains and convulsions, even death in severe cases. An emetic may save the animal in some cases. Salt or dry mustard (1 tablespoon mixed with 1 teaspoonful of water) can be effective in causing vomiting until the veterinarian is reached.

ARTHRITIS—A painful condition of the joints which results in irritation and inflammation. A disease that pretty much confines itself to older dogs, especially in the larger breeds. Limping, irritability and pain are symptomatic. Anti-

Ch. Tamara's Patches of Perse is the dam of nine champions, which makes her the third top-producing bitch in the breed, and was nominated as one of *Popular Dogs* Top Dams. She is now eleven years old, but was one of the first Old English Sheepdogs at Tamara Kennels in Brighton, Michigan, which has produced more than 20 home-bred champions.

inflammatory drugs are effective after X-ray determines the severity. Heat and rest are helpful.

ASCITES—A collection of serous fluid in the abdominal cavity, causing swelling. It may be a result of heavy parasitic infestation or a symptom of liver, kidney, tuberculosis or heart diseases.

ASPERGILLOSIS—A disease contracted from poultry and often mistaken for tuberculosis since symptoms are quite similar. It attacks the nervous system and sometimes has disastrous effects on the respiratory system. This fungus growth in the body tissue spreads quickly and is accompanied by convulsions. The dog rubs his nose and there is a bloody discharge.

ASTHMA—Acute distress in breathing. Attacks may occur suddenly at irregular intervals and last as long as half an hour. The condition may be hereditary or due to allergy or heart condition. Antihistamines are effective in minor attacks.

ATAXIA—Muscular incoordination or lack of movement causing an inhibited gait, although the necessary organs and muscle power are coherent. The dog may have a tendency to stagger.

ATOPY—Manifestations of atopy in the dog are a persistent scratching of the eyes and nose. Onsets are usually seasonal—the dog allergic to, say, ragweed will develop the condition when ragweed is in season, or, say, house dust all year round. Most dogs afflicted with atopy are multi-sensitive and are affected by something several months out of the year. Treatment is by antihistamines or systemic corticosteroids, or both.

— B —

BABESIA GIBSONI (or Babesiosis)—A parasitic disease of the tropics, reasonably rare in the U.S.A. to date. Blood tests can reveal its presence and like other parasitic infections the symptoms are loss of appetite, no pep, anemia and elevations in temperature as the disease advances, and enlarged spleen and liver are sometimes evident.

BALANITIS—The medical term for a constant discharge of pus from the penis which causes spotting of clothing or quarters or causes the dog to clean itself constantly. When bacteria gather at the end of the sheath, it causes irritations in the tissue and pus. If the condition becomes serious, the dog may be cauterized or ointment applied.

BLASTOMYCOSIS—A rare infectious disease involving the kidneys and liver. The animal loses its appetite and vomits. Laboratory examination is necessary to determine presence.

BRADYCARDIA—Abnormal slowness of the heartbeat and pulse.

BRONCHITIS—Inflammation of the mucus lining in the respiratory tract, the windpipe or trachea, and lungs. Dampness and cold are usually responsible and the symptoms usually follow a chill, or may be present with cases of pneumonia or distemper. Symptoms are a nagging dry cough, fever, quickened pulse rate, runny nose, perhaps vomiting, and congested nasal passages which must be kept open. Old dogs are particularly affected. It is a highly transmissible disease and isolation from other animals is important. Antibiotics are given.

BRUCELLA CANIS—An infectious disease associated with abortion in bitches in the last quarter of gestation, sterility or stillbirths. A comparable is testicle trouble in male dogs. It is highly contagious and can be diagnosed through blood tests and animals having the infection should be isolated.

— C —

CANCER (tumors, neoplasia, etc.)—A growth of cells which serve no purpose is referred to as a cancer. The growth may be malignant or benign. Malignancy is the spreading type growth and may invade the entire body. Treatment, if the condition is

At this Specialty Club win at Greenwich, Connecticut in June, 1956 the national event top awards went to (left) the late Mrs. C. M. Crafts, owner-handler of Rosmoore Joy Gift, Best of Opposite Sex, and Mrs. Marvin Kucker (now Mrs. Berkowitz) for the Best of Breed win to her Ch. Merriedip Duke George. Photo by Evelyn Shafer.

diagnosed and caught in time, may be successful by surgical methods, drugs, or radioactive therapy. Haste in consulting your veterinarian cannot be urged too strongly.

CANKER (Otitis)—A bacterial infection of the ear where the ear may drain, have a dreadful odor, and ooze a dark brown substance all the way out to the ear flap. Cause of canker can be from mites, dirt, excessive hair growth in the ear canal, wax, etc. A daily cleaning and administering of antifungal ointment or powder are in order until the condition is cured. Symptoms are the dog shaking his head, scratching his ear and holding the head to the side.

CARIES—A pathologic change causing destruction of the enamel on teeth and subsequent invasion of the dentine; in other words, a cavity in a tooth. This may result in bad breath, toothache, digestive disorders, etc., depending upon the severity. Cavities in dogs are rare, though we hear more and more of false teeth being made for dogs and occasionally even root canal work for show dogs.

CASTRATION—Surgical removal of the male gonads or sex organs. An anesthesia is necessary and the animal must be watched for at least a week to see that hemorrhage does not occur. It is best performed at an early age—anywhere from three to nine months. Older dogs suffering from a hormonal imbalance or cancer of the gonads are castrated.

CATARACT—An opaque growth covering the lens of the eye. Surgical removal is the only treatment. Cataract may be a result of an injury to the eye or in some cases may be an inherited trait.

CELLULITIS—Inflammation of the loose subcutaneous tissue of the body. A condition which can be symptomatic of several other diseases.

CHEILITIS—Inflammation of the lips.

CHOLECYSTITIS—A condition affecting the gall bladder. The onset is usually during the time an animal is suffering from infectious canine hepatitis. Removal of the gall bladder, which thickens and becomes highly vascular, can effect a complete cure.

CHOREA—Brain damage as a result of distemper which has been severe is characterized by convulsive movements of the legs. It is progressive and if it affects the facial muscles, salivating or difficulty in eating or moving the jaws may be evident. Sedatives may bring relief, but this disease is incurable.

CHOROIDITIS—Inflammation of the choroid coat of the eye which is to be regarded as serious. Immediate veterinary inspection is required.

COCCIDIOSIS—An intestinal disease of parasitic nature and origin. Microscopic organisms reproduce on the walls of the intestinal tract and destroy tissue. Bloody diarrhea, loss of weight and appetite and general lethargy result. Presence of parasites is determined by fecal examination. Sulfur drugs are administered and a complete clean up of the premises is in order since the parasite is passed from one dog to another through floor surfaces or eating utensils.

COLOSTRUM—A secretion of the mammary glands for the first day or so after the bitch gives birth. It acts as a purgative for the young, and contains antibodies against distemper, hepatitis and other bacteria.

CONJUNCTIVITIS—Inflammation of the conjunctiva of the eye.

CONVULSIONS—A fit, or violent involuntary contractions of groups of muscles, accompanied by unconsciousness. They are in themselves a symptom of another disease, especially traceable to one affecting the brain; i.e., rabies, or an attack of encephalitis or distemper. It may also be the result of a heavy infestation of parasites or toxic poisonings. Care must be taken that the animal does not injure itself and a veterinarian must be consulted to determine and eliminate the cause.

CRYPTORCHID—A male animal in which neither testicle is present or descended. This condition automatically bars a dog from the show ring.

CYANOSIS—A definite blueness seen in and around the mucous membranes of the face; i.e. tongue, lips and eyes. It is usually synonymous with a circulatory obstruction or heart condition.

CYSTITIS—A disease of the urinary tract which is characterized by inflammation and/or infection in the bladder. Symptoms are straining, frequent urination with little results or with traces of blood, and perhaps a fever. Antibiotics, usually in the sulfur category, as well as antiseptics are administered. This is a condition which is of great discomfort to the animal and is of lengthy duration. Relief must be given by a veterinarian, who will empty bladder by means of catheter or medication to relax the bladder so that the urine may be passed.

— D —

DEMODECTIC MANGE—A skin condition caused by a parasitic mite, *Demodex*, living in hair follicles. This is a difficult condition to get rid of and is treated internally as well as externally. It requires diligent care to free the animal of it entirely.

DERMATITIS—There are many forms of skin irritations and eruptions but perhaps the most common is "contact dermatitis." Redness and itching are present. The irritation is due to something the animal has been exposed to and to which it is allergic. The irritant must be identified and removed. Antihistamines and anti-inflammatory drugs are administered, and in severe cases sedatives or tranquilizers are prescribed to lessen the dog's scratching.

DIABETES (Insipidus)—A deficiency of antidiuretic hormone produced by the posterior pituitary gland. It occurs in older animals and is characterized by the animal's drinking excessive amounts of water and voiding frequently. Treatment is by periodic injection of antidiuretic drug for the rest of the animal's life.

DIABETES (Mellitus)—Sometimes referred to as sugar diabetes, this is a disorder of the metabolism of carbohydrates caused by lack of insulin production by the cells of the pancreas. Symptoms are the same as in the insipidus type, and in severe cases loss of weight, vomiting or coma may occur. Blood and urine analysis confirm its presence. It is treated by low carbohydrate diet, oral medication and/or insulin injections.

DIGITOXIN—A medication given to a dog with congestive heart failure. Dosage is, of course, adjusted to severeness of condition and size of the individual animal.

DISC ABNORMALITIES (Intervertebral)—Between each bone in the spine is a connecting structure called an intervertebral disc. When the disc between two vertebrae becomes irritated and protrudes into the spinal canal it forms lesions and is painful. (This is a disease which particularly affects the Dachshund because of its long back in comparison to length of

The fantastic Ch. Unnesta Pim, imported and shown to a position of top-winning show dog by Barry Goodman, of Bethesda, Maryland. Pim became not only a top-winning show dog in the United States but also a top stud force at Mr. Goodman's famous Rivermist Kennels.

legs.) Paralysis of the legs, reluctance to move, and loss of control of body functions may be symptoms. X-ray and physical examination will determine extent of the condition. Massage helps circulation and pain relievers may be prescribed. Surgery is sometimes successful and portable two-wheel carts which support the hindquarters help.

DISTEMPER—Highly transmissable disease of viral origin which spreads through secretions of nose, eyes or direct oral contact.

May be fatal in puppies under 12 weeks. Symptoms of this disease are alternately high and low fevers, runny eyes and nose, loss of appetite and general lassitude, diarrhea and loss of weight. This disease sometimes goes into pneumonia or convulsions if the virus reaches the brain. Chorea may remain if infection has been severe or neglected. Antibiotics are administered and fluids and sedation may be advised by your veterinarian. If the dog has been inoculated, the disease may remain a light case, BUT it is not to be treated lightly. Warmth and rest are also indicated.

DROPSY—Abnormal accumulation of fluid in the tissues or body cavities. Also referred to as edema when accumulations manifest themselves below the skin. In the stomach region it is called ascites. Lack of exercise or poor circulation, particularly in older dogs, may be the cause. While the swellings are painless, excess accumulations in the stomach can cause digestive distress or heart disturbances, and may be associated with diabetes. Occasional diarrhea, lack of appetite, loss of weight, exhaustion, emaciation and death may occur if the condition is not treated.

DYSGERMINOMA—A malignant ovarian tumor. Symptoms are fever, vaginal discharge, vomiting and diarrhea. Tumors vary in size, though more commonly are on the large size and from reports to date, the right ovary is more commonly affected. Radiotherapy may be successful; if not, surgery is required.

— E —

EAR MANGE—Otodectic mange, or parasitic otitis externa. Ear mites suck lymph fluids through the walls of the ear canal. Infections are high where mites are present and a brownish, horrible smelling ooze is present deep down in the canal all the way out to the flap where the secretion has a granular texture. The dog shakes his head, rubs and scrapes. In extreme cases convulsions or brain damage may result. The ear must be cleaned daily and drugs of an antibiotic and anti-inflammatory nature must be given.

ECLAMPSIA—A toxemia of pregnancy. Shortly after the time a bitch whelps her puppies, her milk may go bad. She will pant as a result of high fever, and go into convulsions. The puppies must be taken away from the mother immediately. This is usually the result of an extreme lack of calcium during pregnancy. Also known as milk fever.

ECTROPION—All breeders of dogs with drooping eyelids or exaggerated haws will be familiar with this condition, where the lower eyelid turns out. It can be a result of an injury, as well as hereditary in some breeds, but can be corrected surgically.

ECZEMA—Eczema is another form of skin irritation which may confine itself to redness and itching, or go all the way to a scaly skin surface or open wet sores. This is sometimes referred to as "hot spots." A hormone imbalance or actual diet deficiency may prevail. Find the cause and remove it. Medicinal baths

From the 1930's comes this photograph of visitors' day at a kennel. Blue Herdsman calls on Blue Boy of Bailcliff at the E. W. Beegles' Kennel in Holicong, Pennsylvania.

and ointments usually provide a cure, but cure is a lengthy process and the condition frequently reoccurs.

EDEMA—Abnormal collection of fluids in the tissues of the body.

ELBOW DYSPLASIA—Term applied to a developmental abnormality of the elbow joints. It is hereditary.

EMPHYSEMA—Labored breathing caused by distended or ruptured lungs. May be acute or chronic and is not uncommon.

EMPYEMA—Accumulation of pus or purulent fluid, in a body cavity, resembling an abscess. Another term for pleurisy.

ENCEPHALITIS—Brain fever associated with meningitis. An inflammation of the brain caused by a virus, rabies or perhaps tuberculosis. It may also be caused by poisonous plants, bad food or lead poisoning. Dogs go "wild," running in circles, falling over, etc. Paralysis and death frequently result. Cure depends on extent of infection and speed with which it is diagnosed and treated.

ENDOCARDITIS—Inflammation and bacterial infection of the smooth membrane that lines the inside of the heart.

ENTERITIS—Intestinal inflammation of serious import. It can be massive or confine itself to one spot. Symptoms are diarrhea, bloody at times, vomiting, and general discomfort. Antibiotics are prescribed and fluids, if the diarrhea and vomiting have been excessive. Causes are varied; may follow distemper or other infections or bacterial infection through intestinal worms.

ENTROPION—A turning in of the margin of the eyelids. As a result, the eyelashes rub on the eyeball and cause irritation resulting in a discharge from the eye. Here again it is a condition peculiar to certain breeds—particularly Chow Chows—or may be the result of an injury which failed to heal properly. Infection may result as the dog will rub his eyes and cause a swelling. It is painful, but can be cured surgically.

ENTEROTOXEMIA—A result of toxins and gases in the intestine. As bacteria increase in the intestine, intermittent diarrhea and/or constipation results from maldigestion. If the infection reaches the kidney through the circulatory system, nephritis results. The digestive system must be cleaned out by use of castor oil or colonic irrigation, and outwardly by

The Winner! American and Canadian Champion Tamara's Shaggy Shoes MacDuff captures another Working Group. This one, owner-handled as usual, was at the Sarnia Kennel Club show in October, 1970. Duffy wound up his show career with 78 Bests of Breed, 31 Group Placings and top OES awards in the United States and Canada. Duffy is owned by Don and Jean McColl of Birmingham, Michigan.

antibiotics.

EOSINOPHILIC MYOSITIS—Inflammation of the muscles dogs use for chewing. Persistent attacks usually lasting one or more weeks. They come and go over long periods of time, coming closer and closer together. Difficulty in swallowing, swelling of the face, or even the dog holding his mouth open will indicate the onset of an attack. Anti-inflammatory drugs are the only known treatment. Cause unknown, outlook grave.

EPILEPSY—The brain is the area affected and fits and/or convulsions may occur early or late in life. It cannot be cured;

however, it can be controlled with medication. Said to be hereditary. Convulsions may be of short duration or the dog may just appear to be dazed. It is rarely fatal. Care must be taken to see that the dog does not injure itself during an attack.

EPIPHORA—A constant tearing which stains the face and fur of dogs. It is a bothersome condition which is not easily remedied either with outside medication or by surgical tear duct removal. There has been some success in certain cases reported from a liquid medication given with the food and prescribed by veterinarians. This condition may be caused by any one or more of a number of corneal irritations, such as nasal malfunction or the presence of foreign matter in the superficial gland of the third eyelid. After complete examination as to the specific cause, a veterinarian can decide whether surgery is indicated.

ESOPHAGEAL DIVERTICULUM—Inflammation or sac-like protrusions on the walls of the esophagus resembling small hernias. It is uncommon in dogs, but operable, and characterized by gagging, listlessness, temperature and vomiting in some cases.

— F —

FALSE PREGNANCY (or pseudopregnancy)—All the signs of the real thing are present in this heart-breaking and frustrating condition. The bitch may even go into false labor near the end of the 63-day cycle and build a nest for her hoped-for puppies. It may be confirmed by X-ray or a gentle feeling for them through the stomach area. Hormones can be injected to relieve the symptoms.

FROSTBITE—Dead tissue as a result of extreme cold. The tissues become red, swollen and painful, and may peel away later, causing open lesions. Ointments and protective coverings should be administered until irritation is alleviated.

FUSOSPIROCHETAL DISEASE—Bad breath is the first and most formidable symptom of this disease of the mouth affecting the gums. Bloody saliva and gingivitus or ulcers in the mouth may also be present, and the dog may be listless due to lack of desire to eat. Cleaning the teeth and gums daily with hydrogen peroxide in prescribed dosage by the veterinarian is required. Further diagnosis of the disease can be confirmed by microscopic examination of smears, though these fusiform bacteria might be present in the mouth of a dog which never becomes infected. Attempts to culture these anaerobes have been unsuccessful.

— G —

GASTRIC DILATION—This is an abnormal swelling of the abdomen due to gas or overeating. Consumption of large amounts of food especially if dry foods are eaten, and then large quantities of water make the dog "swell." The stomach twists so that both ends are locked off. Vomiting is impossible, breathing is hampered and the dog suffers pain until the food is expelled. Dogs that gulp their food and swallow air with it

Fortune's Stepchild out of Old English Sheepdog named Dame Fortune, owned by Mr. and Mrs. Edward Beegle, Holicong, Pennsylvania, whose "reign" dates back to the middle nineteen thirties.

are most susceptible. Immediate surgery may be required to prevent the stomach from bursting. Commonly known as bloat.

GASTRITIS—Inflammation of the stomach caused by many things—spoiled food which tends to turn to gas, overeating, eating foreign bodies, chemicals or even worms. Vomiting is usually the first symptom though the animal will usually drink great quantities of water which more often than not it throws back up. A 24-hour fast which eliminates the cause is the first step toward cure. If vomiting persists chunks of ice cubes put down the throat may help. Hopefully the dog will lick them himself. Keep the dog on a liquid diet for another 24 hours before resuming his regular meals.

GASTRO-ENTERITIS—Inflammation of the stomach and intestines. There is bleeding and ulceration in the stomach and this serious condition calls for immediate veterinary help.

GASTRODUODENITIS—Inflammation of the stomach and duodenum.

GINGIVITIS or gum infection—Badly tartared teeth are usually the cause of this gum infection characterized by swelling, redness at the gum line, bleeding and bloody saliva. Bad breath also. Improper diet may be a cause of it. Feeding of only soft foods as a steady diet allows the tartar to form and to irritate the gums. To effect a cure, clean the teeth and perhaps the veterinarian will also recommend antibiotics.

GLAUCOMA—Pressure inside the eyeball builds up, the eyeball becomes hard and bulgy and a cloudiness of the entire corneal area occurs. The pupil is dilated and the eye is extremely sensitive. Blindness is inevitable unless treatment is prompt at the onset of the disease. Cold applications as well as medical prescriptions are required with also the possibility of surgery, though with no guarantee of success.

GLOSSITIS—Inflammation of the tongue.

GOITER—Enlargement of the thyroid gland, sometimes requiring surgery. In minor cases, medication—usually containing iodine—is administered.

— H —

HARELIP—A malformation of the upper lip characterized by a cleft palate. Difficulty in nursing in exaggerated cases can

On the way to a championship! Pat and Sandi Baker's Droverdale Pride of Polo. This win marked eight points toward the title. Pride was sired by the Bakers' Ch. Droverdale Image of Polo ex Ch. Chadwick's Lady Cricket.

result in starvation or puny development. Operations can be performed late in life.

HEART DISEASE—Heart failure is rare in young dogs, but older dogs which show an unusual heavy breathing after exercise or are easily tired may be victims of heart trouble, and an examination is in order. As it grows worse, wheezing, coughing or gasping may be noticed. Other symptoms indicating faulty circulation may manifest themselves as the animal retains more body fluids as the circulation slows down. Rest, less exercise, and non-fattening diets are advised and medication to remove excess fluids from the body are prescribed. In many cases, doses of digitalis may be recommended.

HEARTWORM *(Dirofilaria immitis)*—This condition does not necessarily debilitate a working dog or a dog that is extremely active. It is diagnosed by a blood test and a microscopic examination to determine the extent of the microfilariae. If positive, further differentials are made for comparison with other microfilariae. Treatment consists of considerable attention to the state of nutrition, and liver and kidney functions are watched closely in older dogs. Medication is usually treatment other than surgery and consists of dithiazine iodine therapy over a period of two weeks. Anorexia and/or fever may occur and supplemental vitamins and minerals may be indicated. Dogs with heavy infestations are observed for possible foreign protein reaction from dying and decomposing worms, and are watched for at least three months.

HEATSTROKE—Rapid breathing, dazed condition, vomiting, temperature, and collapse in hot weather indicate heatstroke. It seems to strike older dogs especially if they are overweight or have indulged in excessive activity. Reduce body temperature immediately by submerging dog in cold water, apply ice packs, cold enemas, etc. Keep dog cool and quiet for at least 24 hours.

HEMATOMA—A pocket of blood that may collect in the ear as a result of an injury or the dog's scratching. Surgery is required to remove the fluid and return skin to cartilage by stitching.

HEMOPHILIA—Excessive bleeding on the slightest provocation. Only male subjects are susceptible and it is a hereditary disease passed on by females. Blood coagulants are now successfully used in certain cases.

HEPATITIS, Infectious canine—This disease of viral nature enters the body through the mouth and attacks primarily the liver. Puppies are the most susceptible to this disease and run a fever and drink excessive amounts of water. Runny eyes, nose, vomiting, and general discomfort are symptoms. In some cases blood builders or even blood transfusions are administered since the virus has a tendency to thin the blood. This depletion of the blood often leaves the dog open to other types of infection and complete recovery is a lengthy process. Antibiotics are usually given and supplemental diet and blood builders are a help. Vaccination for young puppies is essential.

HERNIA (diaphragmatic)—An injury is usually responsible for this separation or break in the wall of diaphragm. Symptoms depend on severity; breathing may become difficult, there is some general discomfort or vomiting. X-rays can determine the extent of damage and the only cure is surgery.

HERNIA (umbilical)—Caused by a portion of the abdominal viscera protruding through a weak spot near the navel. Tendency toward hernia is said to be largely hereditary.

HIP DYSPLASIA or HD is a wearing away of the ball and socket of the hip joint. It is a hereditary disease. The symptoms of this bone abnormality are a limp and an awkwardness in

Two of Tamara Kennels' top producers . . . Ch. Tamara's Patches of Perse, dam of nine champions, and Ch. Tempest of Dalcroy, sire of 21 champions. These two dogs were the basis of Tamara Kennels, owned by Tammy and Marvin Smith of Brighton, Michigan.

raising or lowering the body. X-ray will establish severity and it is wise in buying or selling a dog of any breed to insist on a radiograph to prove the animal is HD clear. The condition can be detected as early as three months and if proven the dog should have as little exercise as possible. There is no cure for this condition. Only pain relievers can be given for the more severe cases. No animal with HD should be used for breeding.

HOOKWORM—Hookworms lodge in the small intestines and suck blood from the intestinal wall. Anemia results from loss of blood. Loss of weight, pale gums, and general weakness are symptoms. Microscopic examination of the feces will determine presence. Emphasis on diet improvement and supplements to build up the blood is necessary and, of course, medication for the eradication of the hookworms. This can be either oral or by veterinary injection.

HYDROCEPHALUS—A condition also known as "water head" since a large amount of fluid collects in the brain cavity, usually before birth. This may result in a difficult birth and the young are usually born dead or die shortly thereafter. Euthanasia is recommended on those that do survive since intelligence is absent and violence to themselves or to others is liable to occur.

HYDRONEPHROSIS—Due to a cystic obstruction the kidney collects urine which cannot be passed through the ureter into the bladder, causing the kidney to swell (sometimes to five times its normal size) and giving pain in the lumbar region. The kidney may atrophy, if the condition goes untreated.

— I —

ICHTHYOSIS—A skin condition over elbows and hocks. Scaliness and cracked skin cover the area particularly that which comes in contact with hard surfaces. Lubricating oils well rubbed into the skin and keeping the animal on soft surfaces are solutions.

IMPETIGO—Skin disease seen in puppies infested by worms, distemper, or teething problems. Little soft pimples cover the surface of the skin. Sulfur ointments and ridding the puppy of the worms are usually sufficient cure as well.

INTERDIGITAL CYSTS—Growths usually found in the toes.

Sadie and Dee . . . better known to Bobtail enthusiasts, as Ch. Sunnybrae Rivermist Gillian and owner Mrs. James W. Mattern of East Lansing, Michigan.

They are painful and cause the dog to favor the paw or not walk on it at all. Surgery is the only cure and antibiotic ointments to keep dirt and infection out are necessary.

INTESTINAL OBSTRUCTIONS—When a foreign object becomes lodged in the intestines and prevents passage of stool constipation results from the blockage. Hernia is another cause of obstruction or stoppage. Pain, vomiting, loss of appetite are symptoms. Fluids, laxatives or enemas should be given to remove blockage. Surgery may be necessary after X-ray determines cause. Action must be taken since death may result from long delay or stoppage.

IRITIS—Inflammation of the iris or colored part of the eye. May be caused by the invasion of foreign bodies or other irritants.

— J —

JAUNDICE—A yellow discoloration of the skin. Liver malfunction causes damage by bile seeping into the circulatory system and being dispensed into the body tissue, causing discoloration of the skin. It may be caused by round worms, liver flukes or gall stones. It may be either acute or chronic and the animal loses ambition, convulses or vomits, sometimes to excess. It may be cured once the cause has been eliminated. Neglect can lead to death.

— K —

KERATITIS—Infection of the cornea of the eye. Distemper or hepatitus may be a cause. Sensitivity to light, watery discharge and pain are symptomatic. Treatment depends on whether the lesion is surface irritation or a puncture of the cornea. Warm compresses may help until the veterinarian prescribes the final treatment. Sedatives or tranquilizers may be prescribed to aid in preventing the dog from rubbing the eye.

KIDNEY WORM—The giant worm that attacks the kidney and kidney tissue. It can reach a yard in length. The eggs of this rare species of worm are passed in the dog's urine rather than the feces. These worms are found in raw fish. It is almost impossible to detect them until at least one of the kidneys is completely destroyed or an autopsy reveals its presence. There is no known cure at this point and, therefore, the only alternative is not to feed raw fish.

— L —

LEAD POISONING—Ingestion of lead-based paints or products such as linoleum containing lead is serious. Symptoms are vomiting, behavior changes and/or hysteria or even convulsions in severe cases. It can be cured by medication if caught early enough. Serious damage can be done to the central nervous system. Blood samples are usually taken to determine amount in the blood. Emetics may be required if heavy intake is determined.

LEPTOSPIROSIS—This viral infection is dangerous and bothersome because it affects many organs of the body before lodging itself in the kidneys. Incubation is about two weeks after exposure to the urine of another affected dog. Temperature, or subtemperature, pain and stiffness in the hindquarters are not uncommon, nor is vomiting. Booster shots after proper vaccination at a young age are usually preventative, but once afflicted, antibiotics are essential to cure.

LOCKJAW (tetanus)—Death rate is very high in this bacterial disease. Puncture wounds may frequently develop into lockjaw. Symptoms are severe. As the disease progresses high fever and stiffness in the limbs become serious though the dog does not lose consciousness. Sedatives must be given to help relax the muscles and dispel the spasms. When the stiffness affects the muscles of the face, intravenous feeding must be provided. If a cure is effected, it is a long drawn out affair. Lockjaw bacteria are found in soil and in the feces of animals and humans.

LYMPHOMA (Hodgkins disease)—Malignant lymphoma most frequently is found in dogs under four years of age, affects the lymph glands, liver and spleen. Anorexia and noticeable loss of weight are apparent as well as diarrhea. Depending on area and organ, discharge may be present. The actual neoplasm or tumorous growth may be surrounded by nodules or neoplastic tissue which should be surgically removed under anesthesia.

— M —

MAMMARY NEOPLASMS—25 per cent of all canine tumors are of mammary origin. About half of all reported cases are benign. They are highly recurrent and, when cancerous, fatalities are high. Age or number of litters has nothing to do with the condition itself or the seriousness.

MANGE—The loss of a patch of hair usually signals the onset of mange, which is caused by any number of types of microscopic mites. The veterinarian will usually take scrapings to determine which of the types it is. Medicated baths and dips plus internal and external medication is essential as it spreads rapidly and with care can be confined to one part cf the body. Antibiotics are prescribed.

MASTITIS (mammary gland infection)—After the birth of her young, a bitch may be beset by an infection causing inflammation of the mammary glands which produce milk for the puppies. Soreness and swelling make it painful for her when the puppies nurse. Abscess may form and she will usually run a fever. Hot compresses and antibiotics are necessary and in some instances hormone therapy.

MENINGITIS—Inflammation affecting the membranes covering the brain and/or spinal cord. It is a serious complication which may result from a serious case of distemper, tuberculosis, hardpad, head injury, etc. Symptoms are delirium, restlessness,

Ch. Beau Chevals Perri-Winkle takes a moment out during grooming to visit the Bichon Frise puppy pen at Beau Cheval Farms in Wycombe, Pennsylvania.

high temperature, and dilated pupils in the eyes. Paralysis and death are almost certain.

METRITIS—This infection, or inflammation of the uterus, causes the dog to exude a bloody discharge. Vomiting and a general lassitude are symptoms. Metritis can occur during the time the bitch is in season or right after giving birth. Antibiotics are used, or in severe cases hysterectomy.

MONORCHIDISM—Having only one testicle.

MOTION SICKNESS—On land, on sea, or in the air, your dog may be susceptible to motion sickness. Yawning, or excessive salivation, may signal the onset, and there is eventual vomiting. One or all of the symptoms may be present and recovery is miraculously fast once the motion ceases. Antinauseant drugs are available for animals which do not outgrow this condition.

MYELOMA—Tumor of the bone marrow. Lameness and evidence of pain are symptoms as well as weight loss, depression and palpable tumor masses. Anemia or unnatural tendency to bleed in severe cases may be observed. The tumors may be detected radiographically, but no treatment has yet been reported for the condition.

— N —

NEONATAL K-9 HERPESVIRUS INFECTION—Though K-9 herpesvirus infection, or CHV, has been thought to be a disease of the respiratory system in adult dogs, the acute necrotizing and hemorraghic disease occurs only in infant puppies. The virus multiplies in the respiratory system and female genital tracts of older dogs. Puppies may be affected in the vaginal canal. Unfortunately the symptoms resemble other neonatal infections, even hepatitis, and only after autopsy can it be detected.

NEPHROTIC SYNDROME—Symptoms may be moist or suppurative dermatitis, edema or hypercholesteremia. It is a disease of the liver and may be the result of another disease. Laboratory data and biopsies may be necessary to determine the actual cause if it is other than renal disease. Cure is effected by eradicating the original disease. This is a relatively uncommon thing in dogs, and liver and urinal function tests are made to determine its presence.

NEURITIS—Painful inflammation of a nerve.

NOSEBLEED (epistaxis)—A blow or other injury which causes injury to the nasal tissues is usually the cause. Tumors, parasites, foreign bodies, such as thorns or burrs or quills, may also be responsible. Ice packs will help stem the tide of blood, though coagulants may also be necessary. Transfusions in severe cases may be indicated.

— O —

ORCHITIS—Inflammation of the testes.

OSTEOGENESIS IMPERFECTA—or "brittle bones" is a condition that can be said to be both hereditary and dietary. It may be due to lack of calcium or phosphorus or both. Radiographs show "thin" bones with deformities throughout the skeleton. Treatment depends on cause.

OSTEOMYELITIS (enostosis)—Bone infection may develop after a bacterial contamination of the bone, such as from a compound fracture. Pain and swelling denote the infection and wet sores may accompany it. Lack of appetite, fever and general inactivity can be expected. Antibiotics are advised after X-ray determines severity. Surgery eliminates dead tissue or bone splinters to hasten healing.

OTITIS—Inflammation of the ear.

— P —

PANCREATITIS—It is difficult to palpate for the pancreas unless it is enlarged, which it usually is if this disease is present. Symptoms to note are as in other gastronomic complaints such as vomiting, loss of appetite, anorexia, stomach pains and general listlessness. This is a disease of older dogs though it has been diagnosed in young dogs as well. Blood, urine and stool examination and observation of the endocrine functions of the dog are in order. Clinical diseases that may result from a serious case of pancreatitis are acute pancreatitis which involves a complete degeneration of the pancreas, atrophy, fibrous and/or neoplasia, cholecystitis. Diabetes mellitus is also a possibility.

PATELLAR LUXATION—"Trick knees" are frequent in breeds that have been "bred down" from Standard to Toy size, and is a condition where the knee bone slips out of position. It is an off again, on again condition that can happen as a result of a jump or excessive exercise. If it is persistent, anti-inflammatory drugs may be given or in some cases surgery can correct it.

PERITONITIS—Severe pain accompanies this infection or inflammation of the lining of the abdominal cavity. Extreme sensitivity to touch, loss of appetite and vomiting occur. Dehydration and weight loss is rapid and anemia is a possibility. Antibiotics should kill the infection and a liquid diet for several days is advised. Painkillers may be necessary or drainage tubes in severe cases.

PHLEBITIS—Inflammation of a vein.

PLACENTA—The afterbirth which accompanies and has been used to nourish the fetus. It is composed of three parts; the chorion, amnion, and allantois.

POLYCYTHEMIA VERA—A disease of the blood causing an elevation of hemoglobin concentration. Blood-letting has been effective. The convulsions that typify the presence can be likened to epileptic fits and last for several minutes. The limbs

Ch. Droverdale Double Trouble, owned by Sue and Wendell Raby. Double Trouble is litter brother to the famous Ch. Droverdale Image of Polo.

are stiff and the body feels hot. Mucous membranes are congested, the dog may shiver, and the skin has a ruddy discoloration. Blood samples must be taken and analyzed periodically. If medication to reduce the production of red blood cells is given, it usually means the dog will survive.

PROCTITIS—Inflammation of the rectum.

PROSTATITIS—Inflammation of the prostate gland.

PSITTACOSIS—This disease which affects birds and people has been diagnosed in rare instances in dogs. A soft, persistent cough indicates the dog has been exposed, and a radiograph will show a cloudy portion on the affected areas of the lung. Antibiotics such as aureomycin have been successful in the known cases and cure has been effected in two to three weeks' time. This is a highly contagious disease, to the point where it can be contracted during a post mortem.

PYOMETRA—This uterine infection presents a discharge of pus from the uterus. High fever may turn to below normal as the infection persists. Lack of appetite with a desire for fluids and frequent urination are evidenced. Antibiotics and hormones are known cures. In severe cases, hysterectomy is done.

— R —

RABIES (hydrophobia)—The most deadly of all dog diseases. The Pasteur treatment is the only known cure for humans. One of the viral diseases that affects the nervous system and damages the brain. It is contracted by the intake, through a bite or cut, of saliva from an infected animal. It takes days or even months for the symptoms to appear, so it is sometimes difficult to locate, or isolate, the source. There are two reactions in a dog to this disease. In the paralytic rabies the dog can't swallow and salivates from a drooping jaw, and progressive paralysis eventually overcomes the entire body. The animal goes into coma and eventually dies. In the furious type of rabies the dog turns vicious, eats strange objects, in spite of a difficulty in swallowing, foams at the mouth, and searches out animals or people to attack—hence the expression "mad dog." Vaccination is available for dogs that run loose. Examination of the brain is necessary to determine actual diagnosis.

RECTAL PROLAPSE—Diarrhea, straining from constipation or heavy infestations of parasites are the most common cause of prolapse which is the expulsion of a part of the rectum through the anal opening. It is cylindrical in shape, and must be replaced within the body as soon as possible to prevent damage. Change in diet, medication to eliminate the cause, etc. will effect a cure.

RETINAL ATROPHY—A disease of the eye that is highly hereditary and may be revealed under ophthalmoscopic examination. Eventual blindness inevitably results. Dogs with retinal atrophy should not be used for breeding. Particularly prominent in certain breeds where current breeding trends have tended to change the shape of the head.

RHINITIS—Acute or chronic inflammation of the mucous membranes of the nasal passages. It is quite common in both dogs and cats. It is seldom fatal, but requires endless "nursing" on the part of the owner for survival, since the nose passages must be kept open so the animal will eat. Dry leather on the nose though there is excessive discharge, high fever, sneezing, etc., are symptoms. Nose discharge may be bloody and the

Princess Jan, the first Sheepdog owned by Beau Cheval Farms, poses at nine years of age with a litter sired by her son, Beau Cheval's Sir Winston. A male from this litter became Champion Beau Chevals Lord Little Chap.

animal will refuse to eat making it listless. The attacks may be recurrent and medication must be administered.

RICKETS—The technical name for rickets is osteomalacia and is due to not enough calcium in the body. The bones soften and the legs become bowed or deformed. Rickets can be cured if caught in early stages by improvement in diet.

RINGWORM—The dread of the dog and cat world! This is a fungus disease where the hair falls out in circular patches. It spreads rapidly and is most difficult to get rid of entirely. Drugs must be administered "inside and out!" The cure takes many weeks and much patience. Ultraviolet lights will show hairs green in color so it is wise to have your animal, or new puppy, checked out by the veterinarian for this disease before introducing him to the household. It is contracted by humans.

ROOT CANAL THERAPY—Injury to a tooth may be treated by prompt dental root canal therapy which involves removal of damaged or necrotic pulp and placing of opaque filling material in the root canal and pulp chamber.

— S —

SALIVARY CYST—Surgery is necessary when the salivary gland becomes clogged or non-functional, causing constant salivation. A swelling becomes evident under the ear or tongue. Surgery will release the accumulation of saliva in the duct of the salivary gland, though it is at times necessary to remove the salivary gland in its entirety. Zygomatic salivary cysts are usually a result of obstructions in the four main pairs of salivary glands in the mouth. Infection is more prevalent in the parotid of the zygomatic glands located at the rear of the mouth, lateral to the last upper molars. Visual symptoms may be protruding eyeballs, pain when moving the jaw, or a swelling in the roof of the mouth. If surgery is necessary, it is done under general anesthesia and the obstruction removed by dissection. Occasionally, the zygomatic salivary gland is removed as well. Stitches or drainage tubes may be necessary or dilation of the affected salivary gland. Oral or internal antibiotics may be administered.

SCABIES—Infection from a skin disease caused by a sarcoptic mange mite.

SCURF (dandruff)—A scaly condition of the body in areas covered with hair. Dead cells combined with dried sweat and sebaceous oil gland materials.

Two great dogs of the mid 1940's have a tug of war. Sunny, whose official name was Blue Boy of Bailcliff, and Shady, whose official name was Sunny's New Lady.

SEBORRHEA—A skin condition also referred to as "stud tail," though studding has nothing to do with the condition. The sebaceous or oil-forming glands are responsible. Accumulation of dry skin, or scurf, is formed by excessive oily deposits while the hair becomes dry or falls out altogether.

SEPTICEMIA—When septic organisms invade the bloodstream, it is called septicemia. Severe cases are fatal as the organisms in the blood infiltrate the tissues of the body and all the body organs are affected. Septicemia is the result of serious wounds, especially joints and bones. Abscess may form. High temperature and/or shivering may herald the onset, and death occurs shortly thereafter since the organisms reproduce and spread rapidly. Close watch on all wounds, antibiotics and sulfur drugs are usually prescribed.

SHOCK (circulatory collapse)—The symptoms and severity of shock vary with the cause and nervous system of the individual dog. Severe accident, loss of blood, and heart failure are the most common cause. Keep the dog warm, quiet and get him to a veterinarian right away. Symptoms are vomiting, rapid pulse, thirst, diarrhea, "cold, clammy feeling" and then eventually physical collapse. The veterinarian might prescribe plasma transfusion, fluids, perhaps oxygen, if pulse continues to be too rapid. Tranquilizers and sedatives are sometimes used as well as antibiotics and steroids. Relapse is not uncommon, so the animal must be observed carefully for several days after initial shock.

SINUSITIS—Inflammation of a sinus gland that inhibits breathing.

SNAKEBITE—The fact must be established as to whether the bite was poisonous or non-poisonous. A horse-shoe shaped double row of toothmarks is a non-poisonous bite. A double, or two-hole puncture, is a poisonous snake bite. Many veterinarians now carry anti-venom serum and this must be injected intramuscularly almost immediately. The veterinarian will probably inject a tranquilizer and other antibiotics as well. It is usually a four-day wait before the dog is normal once again, and the swelling completely gone. During this time the dog should be kept on medication.

SPIROCHETOSIS—Diarrhea which cannot be checked through

normal anti-diarrhea medication within a few days may indicate spirochetosis. While spirochete are believed by some authorities to be present and normal to gastrointestinal tracts, unexplainable diarrhea may indicate its presence in great numbers. Large quantities could precipitate diarrhea by upsetting the normal balance of the organ, though it is possible for some dogs which are infected to have no diarrhea at all.

SPONDYLITIS—Inflammation and loosening of the vertebrae.

STOMATITIS—Mouth infection. Bleeding or swollen gums or excessive salivation may indicate this infection. Dirty teeth are usually the cause. Antibiotics and vitamin therapy are indicated; and, of course, scraping the teeth to eliminate the original cause. See also GINGIVITIS.

STRONGYLIDOSIS—Disease caused by strongyle worms that enter the body through the skin and lodge in the wall of the small intestine. Bloody diarrhea, stunted growth, and thinness are general symptoms, as well as shallow breathing. Heavy infestation or neglect leads to death. Isolation of an affected animal and medication will help eliminate the problem, but the premises must also be cleaned thoroughly since the eggs are passed through the feces.

SUPPOSITORY—A capsule comprised of fat or glycerine introduced into the rectum to encourage defecation. A paper match with the ignitible sulfur end torn off may also be used. Medicated suppositories are also used to treat inflammation of the intestine.

— T —

TACHYCARDIA—An abnormal acceleration of the heartbeat. A rapid pulse signaling a disruption in the heart action. Contact a veterinarian at once.

TAPEWORM—There are many types of tapeworms, the most common being the variety passed along by the flea. It is a white, segmented worm which lives off the wall of the dog's intestine and keeps growing by segments. Some of these are passed and can be seen in the stool or adhering to the hairs on the rear areas of the dog or even in his bedding. It is a difficult worm to get rid of since, even if medication eliminates segments, the head may remain in the intestinal wall to grow again. Symptoms are virtually the same as for other worms:

Debilitation, loss of weight, occasional diarrhea, and general listlessness. Medication and treatment should be under the supervision of a veterinarian.

TETANUS (lockjaw)—A telarius bacillus enters the body through an open wound and spreads where the air does not touch the wound. A toxin is produced and affects the nervous system, particularly the brain or spine. The animal exhibits a stiffness, slows down considerably and the legs may be extended out beyond the body even when the animal is in a standing position. The lips have a twisted appearance. Recovery is rare. Tetanus is not common in dogs, but it can result from a bad job of tail docking or ear cropping, as well as from wounds received by stepping on rusty nails.

THALLOTOXICOSIS or thallium poisoning—Thallium sulfate is a cellular-toxic metal used as a pesticide or rodenticide and a ready cause of poisoning in dogs. Thallium can be detected in the urine by a thallium spot test or by spectrographic analysis by the veterinarian. Gastrointestinal disturbances signal the onset with vomiting, diarrhea, anorexia, stomach cramps. Sometimes a cough or difficulty in breathing occurs. Other intestinal disorders may also manifest themselves as well as convulsions. In mild cases the disease may be simply a skin eruption, depending upon the damage to the kidneys. Enlarged spleens, edema or nephrosis can develop. Antibiotics and a medication called dimercaprol are helpful, but the mortality rate is over 50 per cent.

THROMBUS—A clot in a blood vessel or the heart.

TICK PARALYSIS—Seasonal attacks of ticks or heavy infestations of ticks can result in a dangerous paralysis. Death is a distinct reality at this point and immediate steps must be taken to prevent total paralysis. The onset is observed usually in the hindquarters. Lack of coordination, a reluctance to walk, and difficulty in getting up can be observed. Complete paralysis kills when infection reaches the respiratory system. The paralysis is the result of the saliva of the tick excreted as it feeds.

TOAD POISONING—Some species of toads secrete a potent toxin. If while chasing a toad your dog takes it in his mouth, more than likely the toad will release this toxin from its parotid glands which will coat the mucous membranes of the dog's throat. The dog will salivate excessively, suffer prostration, cardiac arrhythmia. Some tropical and highly toxic species cause convulsions that result in death. Caught in time, there are certain drugs that can be used to counteract the dire effects. Try washing the dog's mouth with large amounts of water and get him to a veterinarian quickly.

TONSILLECTOMY—Removal of the tonsils. A solution called epinephrine, injected at the time of surgery, makes excessive bleeding almost a thing of the past in this otherwise routine operation.

TOXEMIA—The presence of toxins in the bloodstream, which normally should be eliminated by the excretory organs.

TRICHIASIS—A diseased condition of the eyelids, the result of neglect of earlier infection or inflammation.

— U —

UREMIA—When poisonous materials remain in the body, because they are not eliminated through the kidneys, and are recirculated in the bloodstream. A nearly always fatal disease—sometimes within hours—preceded by convulsions and unconsciousness. Veterinary care and treatment are urgent and imperative.

URINARY BLADDER RUPTURE—Injury or pelvic fractures are the most common causes of a rupture in this area. Anuria usually occurs in a few days when urine backs up into the stomach area. Stomach pains are characteristic and a radiograph will determine the seriousness. Bladder is flushed with saline solution and surgery is usually required. Quiet and little exercise is recommended during recovery.

— V —

VENTRICULOCORDECTOMY—Devocalization of dogs, also known as aphonia. In diseases of the larynx this operation may be used. Portions of the vocal cords are removed by manual means or by electrocautery. Food is withheld for a day prior to surgery and premedication is administered. Food is again provided 24 hours after the operation. At the end of three or four months, scar tissue develops and the dog is able to bark in a subdued manner. Complications from surgery are few, but the psychological effects on the animal are to be reckoned with. Suppression of the barking varies from com-

The great Ch. Droverdale Image of Polo, pictured winning his first Best In Show under judge Percy Roberts, and at just 18 months of age.

plete to merely muted, depending on the veterinarian's ability and each individual dog's anatomy.

— W —

WHIPWORMS—Parasites that inhabit the large intestine and the cecum. Two to three inches in length, they appear "whip-like" and symptoms are diarrhea, loss of weight, anemia, restlessness or even pain, if the infestation is heavy enough. Medication is best prescribed by a veterinarian. Cleaning of the kennel is essential, since infestation takes place through the mouth. Whipworms reach maturity within thirty days after intake.

CHAPTER 18

COMPLETE GLOSSARY OF DOG TERMS

ACHILLES HEEL—The major tendon attaching the muscle of the calf from the thigh to the hock

AKC—The American Kennel Club. Address; 51 Madison Avenue, N.Y., N.Y. 10010

ALBINO—Pigment deficiency, usually a congenital fault, which renders skin, hair and eyes pink

AMERICAN KENNEL CLUB—Registering body for canine world in the United States. Headquarters for the stud book, dog registrations, and federation of kennel clubs. They also create and enforce the rules and regulations governing dog shows in the U.S.A.

ALMOND EYE—The shape of the eye opening, rather than the eye itself, which slants upwards at the outer edge, hence giving it an almond shape

ANUS—Anterior opening found under the tail for purposes of alimentary canal elimination

ANGULATION—The angles formed by the meeting of the bones

APPLE-HEAD—An irregular roundedness of topskull. A domed skull

APRON—On long-coated dogs, the longer hair that frills outward from the neck and chest

BABBLER—Hunting dog that barks or howls while out on scent

BALANCED—A symmetrical, correctly proportioned animal; one with correct balance with one part in regard to another

BARREL—Rounded rib section; thorax; chest

BAT EAR—An erect ear, broad at base, rounded or semicircular at top, with opening directly in front

BAY—The howl or bark of the hunting dog

BEARD—Profuse whisker growth

BEAUTY SPOT—Usually roundish colored hair on a blaze of another color. Found mostly between the ears

The Reverend William Buchanan with a Welsh Corgi and an Old English Sheepdog owned by Mrs. Edward P. Renner of Great Barrington, Mass. The Rev. Buchanan was photographed in full Scottish kilt by Percy T. Jones at the 2nd Annual dog show of the Northwestern Connecticut Dog Club in August, 1947.

BEEFY—Overdevelopment or overweight in a dog, particularly hindquarters

BELTON—A color designation particularly familiar to Setters. An intermingling of colored and white hairs

BITCH—The female dog

BLAZE—A type of marking. White stripe running up the center of the face between the eyes

BLOCKY—Square head

BLOOM—Dogs in top condition are said to be "in full bloom"

BLUE MERLE—A color designation. Blue and gray mixed with black. Marbled-like appearance

BOSSY—Overdevelopment of the shoulder muscles

BRACE—Two dogs which move as a pair in unison

BREECHING—Tan-colored hair on inside of the thighs

BRINDLE—Even mixture of black hairs with brown, tan or gray

BRISKET—The forepart of the body below the chest

BROKEN COLOR—A color broken by white or another color

BROKEN-HAIRED—A wiry coat

BROKEN-UP FACE—Receding nose together with deep stop, wrinkle, and undershot jaw

BROOD BITCH—A female used for breeding

BRUSH—A bushy tail

BURR—Inside part of the ear which is visible to the eye

BUTTERFLY NOSE—Parti-colored nose or entirely flesh color

BUTTON EAR—The edge of the ear which folds to cover the opening of the ear

CANINE—Animals of the Canidae family which includes not only dogs but foxes, wolves, and jackals

CANINES—The four large teeth in the front of the mouth often referred to as fangs

CASTRATE—The surgical removal of the testicles on the male dog

CAT-FOOT—Round, tight, high-arched feet said to resemble those of a cat

CHARACTER—The general appearance or expression said to be typical of the breed

CHEEKY—Fat cheeks or protruding cheeks

CHEST—Forepart of the body between the shoulder blades and above the brisket

CHINA EYE—A clear blue wall eye

CHISELED—A clean cut head, especially when chiseled out below the eye

CHOPS—Jowls or pendulous lips

CLIP—Method of trimming coats according to individual breed standards

CLODDY—Thick set or plodding dog

CLOSE-COUPLED—A dog short in loins; comparatively short from withers to hipbones

COBBY—Short-bodied; compact

COLLAR—Usually a white marking, resembling a collar, around the neck

CONDITION—General appearance of a dog showing good health, grooming and care

CONFORMATION—The form and structure of the bone or framework of the dog in comparison with requirements of the Standard for the breed

CORKY—Active and alert dog

COUPLE—Two dogs

COUPLING—Leash or collar-ring for a brace of dogs

COUPLINGS—Body between withers and the hipbones indicating either short or long coupling

COW HOCKED—When the hocks turn toward each other and sometimes touch

CRANK TAIL—Tail carried down

CREST—Arched portion of the back of the neck

CROPPING—Cutting or trimming of the ear leather to get ears to stand erect

CROSSBRED—A dog whose sire and dam are of two different breeds

CROUP—The back part of the back above the hind legs. Area from hips to tail

CROWN—The highest part of the head; the topskull

CRYPTORCHID—Male dog with neither testicle visible

CULOTTE—The long hair on the back of the thighs

CUSHION—Fullness of upper lips

DAPPLED—Mottled marking of different colors with none predominating

DEADGRASS—Dull tan color

DENTITION—Arrangement of the teeth

DEWCLAWS—Extra claws, or functionless digits on the inside of the four legs; usually removed at about three days of age

DEWLAP—Loose, pendulous skin under the throat

DISH-FACED—When nasal bone is so formed that nose is higher at the end than in the middle or at the stop

DISQUALIFICATION—A dog which has a fault making it ineligible to compete in dog show competition

DISTEMPER TEETH—Discolored or pitted teeth as a result of having had Distemper

DOCK—To shorten the tail by cutting

DOG—A male dog, though used freely to indicate either sex

DOMED—Evenly rounded in topskull; not flat but curved upward

DOWN-FACED—When nasal bone inclines toward the tip of the nose

DOWN IN PASTERN—Weak or faulty pastern joints; a let-down foot

DROP EAR—The leather pendant which is longer than the leather of the button ear

DRY NECK—Taut skin

DUDLEY NOSE—Flesh-colored or light brown pigmentation in the nose

ELBOW—The joint between the upper arm and the forearm

ELBOWS OUT—Turning out or off the body and not held close to the sides

EWE NECK—Curvature of the top of neck

EXPRESSION—Color, size and placement of the eyes which give the dog the typical expression associated with his breed

FAKING—Changing the appearance of a dog by artificial means to make it more closely resemble the Standard. White chalk to whiten white fur, etc.

FALL—Hair which hangs over the face

FEATHERING—Longer hair fringe on ears, legs, tail, or body

FEET EAST AND WEST—Toes turned out

FEMUR—The large heavy bone of the thigh

FIDDLE FRONT—Forelegs out at elbows, pasterns close, and feet turned out

FLAG—A long-haired tail

FLANK—The side of the body between the last rib and the hip

FLARE—A blaze that widens as it approaches the topskull

FLAT BONE—When girth of the leg bones is correctly elliptical rather than round

FLAT-SIDED—Ribs insufficiently rounded as they meet the breastbone

FLEWS—Upper lips, particularly at inner corners

FOREARM—Bone of the foreleg between the elbow and the pastern

FOREFACE—Front part of the head; before the eyes; muzzle

FROGFACE—Usually overshot jaw where nose is extended by the receding jaw

FRINGES—Same as feathering

FRONT—Forepart of the body as viewed head-on

FURROW—Slight indentation or median line down center of the skull to the top

GAY TAIL—Tail carried above the top line

GESTATION—The period during which bitch carries her young; 63 days in the dog

GOOSE RUMP—Too steep or sloping a croup

GRIZZLE—Blueish-gray color

GUN-SHY—When a dog fears gun shots

GUARD HAIRS—The longer stiffer hairs which protrude through the undercoat

HARD-MOUTHED—The dog that bites or leaves tooth marks on the game he retrieves

HARE-FOOT—A narrow foot

HARLEQUIN—A color pattern, patched or pied coloration, predominantly black and white

HAW—A third eyelid or membrane at the inside corner of the eye

HEEL—The same as the hock

HEIGHT—Vertical measurement from the withers to the ground; or shoulder to the ground

HOCK—The tarsus bones of the hind leg which form the joint between the second thigh and the metatarsals.

HOCKS WELL LET DOWN—When distance from hock to the ground is close to the ground

HOUND—Dogs commonly used for hunting by scent

HOUND-MARKED—Three-color dogs; white, tan and black, predominating color mentioned first

HUCKLEBONES—The top of the hipbones

HUMERUS—The bone of the upper arm

INBREEDING—The mating of closely related dogs of the same standard, usually brother to sister

Ch. Prospectblue Samuel, owned by Dr. and Mrs. Hugh Jordan of the Loyalblu Kennels, Reg. of Whittier, California.

INCISORS—The cutting teeth found between the fangs in the front of the mouth

ISABELLA—Fawn or light bay color

KINK TAIL—A tail which is abruptly bent appearing to be broken

KNUCKLING-OVER—An insecurely knit pastern jöint often causes irregular motion while dog is standing still

LAYBACK—Well placed shoulders

LAYBACK—Receding nose accompanied by an undershot jaw

LEATHER—The flap of the ear

LEVEL BITE—The front or incisor teeth of the upper and low jaws meet exactly

LINE BREEDING—The mating of related dogs of the same breed to a common ancestor. Controlled inbreeding. Usually grandmother to grandson, or grandfather to granddaughter.

LIPPY—Lips that do not meet perfectly

LOADED SHOULDERS—When shoulder blades are out of alignment due to overweight or overdevelopment on this particular part of the body

LOIN—The region of the body on either side of the vertebral column between the last ribs and the hindquarters

LOWER THIGH—Same as second thigh

LUMBER—Excess fat on a dog

LUMBERING—Awkward gait on a dog

MANE—Profuse hair on the upper portion of neck

MANTLE—Dark-shaded portion of the coat or shoulders, back and sides

MASK—Shading on the foreface

MEDIAN LINE—Same as furrow

MOLERA—Abnormal ossification of the skull

MONGREL—Puppy or dog whose parents are of two different breeds

MONORCHID—A male dog with only one testicle apparent

MUZZLE—The head in front of the eyes—this includes nose, nostrils and jaws as well as the foreface

MUZZLE-BAND—White markings on the muzzle

MOLAR—Rear teeth used for actual chewing

NOSLIP RETRIEVER—The dog at heel—and retrieves game on command

NOSE—Scenting ability

NICTITATING EYELID—The thin membrane at the inside corner of the eye which is drawn across the eyeball. Sometimes referred to as the third eyelid

OCCIPUT—The upper crest or point at the top of the skull

OCCIPITAL PROTUBERANCE—The raised occiput itself

OCCLUSION—The meeting or bringing together of the upper and lower teeth.

OLFACTORY—Pertaining to the sense of smell

OTTER TAIL—A tail that is thick at the base, with hair parted on under side

OUT AT SHOULDER—The shoulder blades are set in such a manner that the joints are too wide, hence jut out from the body

OUTCROSSING—The mating of unrelated individuals of the same breed

OVERHANG—A very pronounced eyebrow

OVERSHOT—The front incisor teeth on top overlap the front teeth of the lower jaw. Also called pig jaw

PACK—Several hounds kept together in one kennel

PADDLING—Moving with the forefeet wide, to encourage a body roll motion

PADS—The underside, or soles, of the feet

PARTI-COLOR—Variegated in patches of two or more colors

PASTERN—The collection of bones forming the joint between the radius and ulna, and the metacarpals

PEAK—Same as occiput

PENCILING—Black lines dividing the tan colored hair on the toes

PIED—Comparatively large patches of two or more colors. Also. called parti-colored or piebald

PIGEON-BREAST—A protruding breastbone

PIG JAW—Jaw with overshot bite

PILE—The soft hair in the undercoat

PINCER BITE—A bite where the incisor teeth meet exactly

PLUME—A feathered tail which is carried over the back

POINTS—Color on face, ears, legs and tail in contrast to the rest of the body color

POMPON—Rounded tuft of hair left on the end of the tail after clipping

PRICK EAR—Carried erect and pointed at tip

PUPPY—Dog under one year of age

Ch. Droverdale Foggy Day pictured at 13 months of age. Foggy Day is the only bitch to finish undefeated at just 13 months. She is owned by Pat and Sandi Baker of Oxon Hill, Maryland, owners of the Droverdale Kennels. Photo by Twomey.

QUALITY—Refinement, fineness

QUARTERS—Hind legs as a pair

RACY—Tall, of comparatively slight build

RAT TAIL—The root thick and covered with soft curls—tip devoid of hair or having the appearance of having been clipped

RINGER—A substitute for close resemblance

RING TAIL—Carried up and around and almost in a circle

ROACH BACK—Convex curvature of back

ROAN—A mixture of colored hairs with white hairs. Blue roan, orange roan, etc.

ROMAN NOSE—A nose whose bridge has a convex line from forehead to nose tip. Ram's nose

ROSE EAR—Drop ear which folds over and back revealing the burr

ROUNDING—Cutting or trimming the ends of the ear leather

RUFF—The longer hair growth around the neck

SABLE—A lacing of black hair in or over a lighter ground color

SADDLE—A marking over the back, like a saddle

SCAPULA—The shoulder blade

SCREW TAIL—Naturally short tail twisted in spiral formation

SCISSORS BITE—A bite in which the upper teeth just barely overlap the lower teeth

SELF COLOR—One color with lighter shadings

SEMIPRICK EARS—Carried erect with just the tips folding forward

SEPTUM—The line extending vertically between the nostrils

SHELLY—A narrow body which lacks the necessary size required by the Breed Standard

SICKLE TAIL—Carried out and up in a semicircle

SLAB SIDES—Insufficient spring of ribs

SLOPING SHOULDER—The shoulder blade which is set obliquely or "laid back"

SNIPEY—A pointed nose

SNOWSHOE FOOT—Slightly webbed between the toes

SOUNDNESS—The general good health and appearance of a dog in its entirety

SPAYED—A female whose ovaries have been removed surgically

SPECIALTY CLUB—An organization to sponsor and promote an individual breed

SPECIALTY SHOW—A dog show devoted to the promotion of a single breed

SPECTACLES—Shading or dark markings around the eyes or from eyes to ears

SPLASHED—Irregularly patched, color on white or vice versa

SPLAY FOOT—A flat or open-toed foot

SPREAD—The width between the front legs

SPRING OF RIBS—The degree of rib roundness

SQUIRREL TAIL—Carried up and curving slightly forward

STANCE—Manner of standing

STARING COAT—Dry harsh hair; sometimes curling at the tips

STATION—Comparative height of a dog from the ground—either high or low

STERN—Tail of a sporting dog or hound

STERNUM—Breastbone

STIFLE—Joint of hind leg between thigh and second thigh. Sometimes called the ham

STILTED—Choppy, up-and-down gait of straight-hocked dog

STOP—The step-up from nose to skull between the eyes

STRAIGHT-HOCKED—Without angulation; straight behind

SUBSTANCE—Good bone. Or in good weight, or well muscled dog

SUPERCILIARY ARCHES—The prominence of the frontal bone of the skull over the eye

SWAYBACK—Concave curvature of the back between the withers and the hipbones

TEAM—Four dogs usually working in unison

THIGH—The hindquarter from hip joint to stifle

THROATINESS—Excessive loose skin under the throat

THUMB-MARKS—Black spots in the tan markings on the pasterns

TICKED—Small isolated areas of black or colored hairs on a white background

TIMBER—Bone, especially of the legs

TOPKNOT—Tuft of hair on the top of head

TRIANGULAR EYE—The eye set in surrounding tissue of triangular shape. A three-cornered eye

TRI-COLOR—Three colors on a dog, white, black and tan

TRUMPET—Depression or hollow on either side of the skull just behind the eye socket; comparable to the temple area in man

TUCK-UP—Body depth at the loin

TULIP EAR—Ear carried erect with slight forward curvature along the sides

TURN-UP—Uptilted jaw

TYPE—The distinguishing characteristics of a dog to measure its worth against the Standard for the breed

UNDERSHOT—The front teeth of the lower jaw overlapping or projecting beyond the front teeth of the upper jaw

UPPER-ARM—The humerus bone of the foreleg between the shoulder blade and forearm

VENT—Tan-colored hair under the tail

WALLEYE—A blue eye also referred to as a fish or pearl eye

WEAVING—When the dog is in motion, the forefeet or hind feet cross

WEEDY—A dog too light of bone

WHEATEN—Pale yellow or fawn color

WHEEL-BACK—Back line arched over the loin; roach back

WHELPS—Unweaned puppies

WHIP TAIL—Carried out stiffly straight and pointed

WIRE-HAIRED—A hard wiry coat

WITHERS—The peak of the first dorsal vertebra; highest part of the body just behind the neck

WRINKLE—Loose, folding skin on forehead and/or foreface

CHAPTER 19

PURSUING A CAREER IN DOGS

One of the biggest joys for those of us who love dogs is to see someone we know or someone in our family grow up in the fancy and go on to enjoy the sport of dogs in later life. Many dog lovers, in addition to leaving codicils in wills, are providing for veterinary scholarships for deserving youngsters who wish to make their association with dogs their vocation.

Unfortunately, many children who have this earnest desire are not always able to afford the expense of an education that will take them through veterinary school, and they are not eligible for scholarships. In recent years, however, we have had a great innovation in this field—a college course for those interested in earning an Animal Science degree, which costs less than half of what it costs to complete veterinary courses. These students have been a boon to veterinarians, and a number of colleges are now offering the program.

Any one who has crossed the threshold of a veterinarian's office during the past decade will readily concur that, with each passing year, the waiting rooms become more crowded and the demands on the doctor's time for research, consultation, surgery and treatment are consuming more and more of the working hours over and above regular office hours. The tremendous increase in the number of dogs and cats and other domestic animals, both in cities and in the suburbs, has resulted in an almost overwhelming consumption of our time.

Until recently most veterinary help consisted of kennel men or women who were restricted to services more properly classified as office maintenance rather than actual veterinary assistance. Needless to say, their part in the operation of a veterinary office is both essential and appreciated; as are the endless details and volumes of paper work capably handled by office secretaries and receptionists.

Ivan Forbes' great Best In Show-winning Old English, Ch. Duke of Fuzzbuzz, winning this time at the Battle Creek Kennel Club in August, 1969 under judge Gerhard Plaga. Photo by Frank.

However, still more of the veterinarian's duties could be handled by properly trained semiprofessionals.

With exactly this service in mind, several colleges are now conducting two-year courses in Animal Science for the training of such semiprofessionals, thereby opening an entire new field for animal technologists. The time saved by the assistance of these trained semiprofessionals will relieve veterinarians of the more mechanical chores and will allow them more time for diagnosing and general servicing of their clients.

"Delhi Tech," the State University Agricultural and Technical College at Delhi, New York, has already graduated several classes of those technologists, and many other institutions of learning are offering comparable two-year courses at the college level. Entry requirements are usually that each applicant must be a graduate of an approved high school, or take the State University Admissions Examination. In addition, each applicant for the Animal Science

Technology program must have some previous credits in mathematics and science, with chemistry an important part of the science background.

The program at Delhi was a new educational venture dedicated to the training of competent technicians for employment in the biochemical field and has been generously supported by a five-year grant, designated as a "Pilot Development Program in Animal Science." This grant has provided both personnel and scientific equipment with obvious good results, while being performed pursuant to a contract with the United States Department of Health, Education and Welfare. Delhi is a unit of the State University of New York and is accredited by the Middle States Association of Colleges and Secondary Schools. Their campus provides offices, laboratories and animal quarters, and they are equipped with modern instruments to train their technicians in laboratory animal care, physiology, pathology, microbiology, anesthesia, X-ray and germ-free techniques. Sizeable animal colonies are maintained in airconditioned quarters, and include mice, rats, hamsters, guinea-pigs, gerbils and rabbits, as well as dogs and cats.

First year students are given such courses as Livestock Pro-

Bernadette Roeder of Mechanicsburg, Pennsylvania, poses with her two male Sheepdogs, Beau Chevals Honey Fitz and their newest arrival from Beau Cheval Farms.

Robert Yetter's Beau Cheval's Bunny Rose, sired by Beau Cheval's Sir Winston out of Princess Jan. Bunny was bred by Marlene J. Anderson and reigns supreme at the Yetter home in Collegeville, Pennsylvania.

duction, Dairy Food Science, General, Organic and Biological Chemistry, Mammalian Anatomy, Histology, and Physiology, Pathogenic Microbiology, Quantitative and Instrumental Analysis, to name a few. Second year students matriculate in General Pathology, Animal Parasitology, Animal Care and Anesthesia, Introductory Psychology, Animal Breeding, Animal Nutrition, Hematology and Urinalysis, Radiology, Genetics, Food Sanitation and Meat Inspection, Histological Techniques, Animal Laboratory Practices and Axenic Techniques. These, of course, may be supplemented by electives that prepare the student for contact with the public in the administration of these duties. Such recommended electives include Public Speaking, Botany, Animal Reproduction and other related subjects.

In addition to Delhi, there are at least a dozen other schools, in California, Maine and Maryland, now offering training for animal technologists. Students at the State University of Maine, for instance, receive part of their practical training at the Animal Medical Center in New York City, under the tutelage of Dr. Robert Tashjian and his highly qualified staff. Dr. John R. McCoy,

A captivating head study shot of Beau Cheval Shango, which so typifies the Old English's "shaggy dog" image! Shango possesses the much desired dark eyerims and was pointed at one year of age. Shango is an active stud at the Beau Cheval kennels.

Secretary of the New Jersey Veterinary Medical Association, recently petitioned Rutgers University, on behalf of the veterinaries of the state, for the development of just such a college program. It is hoped that more and more states will follow this lead since the need is immediate in the animal technology field. Veterinarians are most enthusiastic about the possibilities offered by these new resources being made available to our profession.

Under direct veterinary supervision, the following duties are just some of the procedures in an animal hospital that can be executed by the semiprofessional.

- Recording of vital information relative to a case. This would include such information as the client's name, address, telephone number and other facts pertinent to the visit. The case history would include the breed, age of the animal, its sex, temperature, previous client, etc.
- Preparation of the animal for surgery.
- Preparation of equipment and medicaments to be used in surgery.
- Preparation of medicaments for dispensing to cilents on prescription of the attending veterinarian.
- Administration and application of certain medicines.
- Administration of colonic irrigations.
- Application or changing of wound dressings.

Beau Cheval Agnes, a 10-week-old puppy owned by J. English, III, of New Haven, Connecticut.

- Cleaning of kennels, exercise runs and kitchen utensils.
- Preparation of food and the feeding of patients.
- Explanation to clients on the handling and restraint of their pets, including needs for exercise, house training and elementary obedience training.
- First-aid treatment for hemorrhage, including the proper use of tourniquets.
- Preservation of blood, urine and pathologic material for the purpose of sending them to a laboratory.
- General care and supervision of the hospital or clinic patients to insure their comfort.
- Nail trimming and grooming of patients.

High school graduates with a sincere affection and regard for animals, and a desire to work with veterinarians and perform such clinical duties will fit in especially well. Women particularly will be useful since, over and beyond the strong maternal instinct that goes so far in the care and the "recovery" phase when dealing with animals, women will find the majority of their duties well within not only their mental—but their physical—capabilities. Since a majority of the positions will be in the small animal field, their dexterity will also fit in very well. Students, with financial restrictions that preclude their education and licensing as full-fledged veterinarians, can in this way pursue careers in an area that is close to their actual desire. Their assistance in the pharmaceutical field, where drug concerns deal with laboratory animals, covers another wide area for trained assistance. The career opportunities are varied and reach into job opportunities in medical centers, research institutions and government health agencies; and the demand for graduates far exceeds the current supply of trained personnel.

As far as the financial remunerations, yearly salaries are estimated at an average of $5000 as a starting point. As for the estimate of basic college education expenses, they range from $1800 to $2200 per year for out-of-state residents, and include tuition, room and board, college fees, essential textbooks and limited personal expenses. These personal expenses, of course, will vary with individual students.

Veterinary Councils all over the country are discussing ways they can help and are offering suggestions and opinions on the training of these semiprofessionals.

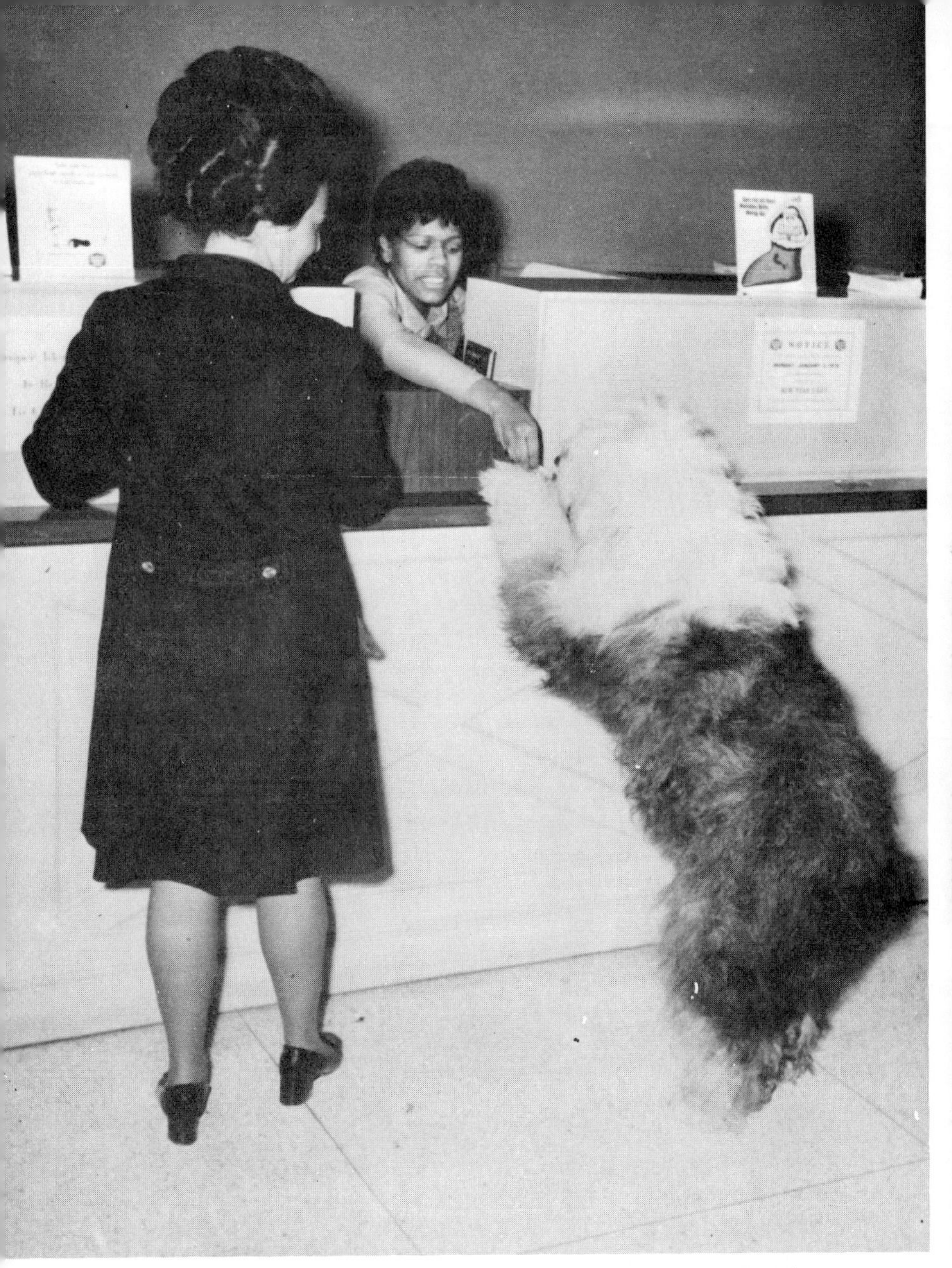

Mrs. Shirley Felinton of Ridley Park, Pennsylvania, always takes her Old English Sheepdog, Mazzie, to the bank each week. Mazzie became such a favorite with teller Mrs. Myra Burnley at the Southeast National Bank's Ridley Township office that Mrs. Burnley has a dog biscuit for her on each visit. Mazzie has gotten to know exactly which window to go to get her "withdrawal"!

INDEX

D

E

F

G

H

I

J

U

V

W

Y